Practical Guide to Managing People

Practical Guide to Managing People

EUGENE RICHMAN
ARVINDER BRARA

Parker Publishing Company, Inc.   West Nyack, New York

Library of Congress Cataloging in Publication Data

Richman, Eugene.
   Practical guide to managing people.

   Includes bibliographical references.
   1. Supervision of employees. 2. Personnel manage-
ment. I. Brara, Arvinder,   joint author.
II. Title.
HF5549.R53   658.3'02   75-1464
ISBN 0-13-690958-2

HOW THIS BOOK WILL HELP YOU GET THINGS DONE THROUGH PEOPLE

As a manager you have to deal with people constantly. Therefore, learning how to motivate and manage people is the most essential task facing you. This book is aimed at providing you with an insight into the behavior of people in organizations. It deals specifically with how to motivate and manage your subordinates, peers and seniors to help accomplish your personal and organizational objectives.

This is a practical book based on many years of experience in working with people in small as well as large organizations. It aims at being a guide for persons in important management positions to examine their performance in dealing with people, to help diagnose their weaknesses and to improve their effectiveness. For younger persons in management—and for those who plan to make it their career—this book should provide both a vision of what organizational behavior is, in actual practice, and concrete guidance for managing people successfully.

Important concepts and methods for understanding and managing people have been illustrated by actual instances in the form of case examples. The numerous examples used are aimed at showing how various approaches and techniques can be applied in practice. The necessary step-wise procedures have been listed to facilitate the application of specific techniques.

Each chapter in the book covers a significant area of dealing with and managing people. The earlier chapters cover the identification of objectives and understanding employee behavior and motivation. Subsequent chapters cover different facets of managing people. The latter chapters deal with accomplishing things through people under difficult situations. We would suggest that while going through each chapter you consider your own performance in the particular aspect being covered and see how your effectiveness can be improved by using the approaches and techniques outlined. This will not only help you to increase your understanding of organizational behavior but aid you in applying these approaches and techniques in motivating and managing people.

Among the areas covered are: how to set objectives in your group, how to make your employees more creative, how to instruct and inform your people, how to get the best results from your people, how to help those in higher ranks to help you and how to accomplish more through others.

The latter four chapters of the book are designed to help provide you with methods and techniques to get the most out of difficult and unusual situations. You will get an insight into such matters as, how to get the most from natural competition, how to minimize people's resistance to change, how to keep control in crises situations, etc.

Some of the important topics covered in different chapters are minimizing conflict and stress in your group, improving the climate for creativity among your people, cultivating your boss, etc. These are topics which every manager is interested in and directly concerned with but seldom gets to form a predetermined strategy and approach toward. This book will help you to learn about the tried and successful approaches and techniques which can be used in relation to the above situations.

Footnotes, acknowledgements and other references have been avoided throughout, except where they are likely to be helpful in providing information about books that give detailed treatment to some of the related topics touched upon in this book.

Experience shows that the fundamental principles and general framework of the approaches and techniques discussed in the following pages prove to be broadly applicable in helping managers to improve their ability to manage people. However, these approaches and techniques can be further refined and adapted by you to better suit your own particular situation and organization. This book poses no additional work. On the contrary, it is aimed to help you to do your job with less stress and greater effectiveness.

It is our hope that by applying these approaches and techniques you can understand your people better and motivate them to become better employees in the process of achieving your managerial objectives successfully.

Eugene Richman
Arvinder Brara

CONTENTS

13

3. SETTING OBJECTIVES IN YOUR GROUP *(Con't)*

4. HOW TO MAKE YOUR EMPLOYEES MORE CREATIVE 64

5. HOW TO INSTRUCT AND INFORM YOUR PEOPLE 88

6. HOW TO GET THE BEST RESULTS FROM YOUR PEOPLE 98

Chapter 1

HOW TO IDENTIFY
YOUR OBJECTIVES

To be a successful manager, you need to be clear about the objectives you want to achieve through managing people. These would include your personal objectives as well as the objectives of your organization. You must recognize the conflicts and similarities between your own objectives and those of your firm's, and how the differences can be smoothed out. Let us see how this can be done.

YOUR PERSONAL OBJECTIVES

The origin of anybody's personal objectives is complex. Your personal objectives in the business world arise out of the following two basic needs of all human beings:

1. A need to survive and improve your standard of living.
2. A need to demonstrate and develop your natural capacities and skills.

Any manager's personal objectives seek to satisfy his personal needs for money, status, social esteem, achievement, power, excellence, etc. Since money often leads to status and social esteem, your personal objectives will tend to center on economic advancement through a promotion, salary raise, transfer to a better job, etc. However, observers have discovered that as the need for money is satisfied more and more, the needs for achievement, power and excellence become more important.

Your personal objectives are dynamic in several senses:
1. With time, the priorities of your objectives shift, due to changes within yourself and changes in your environment.
2. Once you have reached a particular objective, you either reduce your efforts, or direct your attention toward other objectives and shift your priorities.
3. When you interact with others, as in a work situation, your experience can alter your individual objectives and priorities, as well as theirs.
4. Clear objectives stimulate accomplishment.

Thus, your personal objectives, especially short range ones, are always in a state of flux. They are affected by your work group, subordinates, your boss and other factors in the environment. As a manager, you need to continuously define your personal objectives clearly for efficient accomplishment. Starting from the long range objectives, you should set some personal targets to be accomplished in the next fifteen years or so. You may set your objectives at different levels for 3, 5, 10 and 15 year periods to suit your own pace and particular situation. For example, as a manager you may like to set, as an objective, a promotion in the next two years, or qualifying for a particular position you want in the next three years, etc.

To achieve this goal you will have to set shorter range goals, which will be molded by the particular work situation you are in. You might have to achieve certain organizational goals, sort out personnel conflicts, strengthen your work team, increase the output from your subordinates, introduce desirable changes, get your superiors to accept your potential, manage problem people, etc. For accomplishing these objectives, you and you alone are in the best position to set specific goals for yourself. You have to decide what needs to be done in the short range to help you achieve your long range personal objectives.

Whatever the nature or whim of your personal objectives, often the only major source of achieving them is by being successful in the organizational framework. To be successful in the organizational framework, you need to understand and identify with organizational objectives.

YOUR ORGANIZATION'S OBJECTIVES

Whatever the ultimate objectives of your business organization may be, its basic fundamental objective is economic performance. Economic performance is not only the specific function and contribution of business performance, but the very reason for its existence.[1] Thus both the long term and short term objectives of your organization depend upon its economic performance within its social constraints.

Your company may state that its objectives are organizational growth, leadership in industry, social recognition, etc., but these can only be achieved within the successful economic operation of the enterprise. Since your company's objectives are to be achieved through its managers, you, like the other managers, have to be concerned with the successful economic contribution of your respective organizational unit.

DIFFERENCES BETWEEN YOUR ORGANIZATIONAL AND PERSONAL OBJECTIVES

Your personal objectives as a manager are linked with your company's organizational objectives only through the organizational unit which you manage. The average manager tries to maximize the net economic performance of his department or unit. This departmental goal may not conform to the organization's overall objectives. Thus, a production manager may order long production runs to decrease the per unit cost of his production. If the resulting inventory storage costs are excessively high, though, the overall company profit will be lower. The production manager in such a situation would achieve his *departmental objective* of reducing manufacturing costs per unit, but would lessen overall organizational efficiency. On the other hand, a production manager who plans production runs so that the total company's profit is improved—even with a slight rise in the production cost per unit—is the manager who is doing the right thing in his organizational context. This manager is likely to climb up the

---

[1] Peter Drucker, The Effective Executive, William Heineman, Ltd., London, 1967.

ladder of success faster than the one who restricts his approach to the achievement of his department's objectives alone.

There will always be such conflicts and differences between your personal objectives of increasing your unit's efficiency, and the overall company's economic objectives. Under such conditions, you have to focus first on the overall organizational objectives, and bring your unit's objectives in line with them. In other words, the manager must always attempt to maximize his unit's contribution to the organization, rather than maximize his unit's performance without regard to its possible adverse impact on the overall organization.

HOW YOU CAN SMOOTH OUT DIFFERENCES IN OBJECTIVES

To smooth out the differences between your personal and organizational objectives, you have to focus on the *contribution,* rather than on the *skills* and *techniques,* of the work you are doing. Skills and techniques are important only in the context of the contribution which you, the manager, can make to the overall organization. Therefore, you have to first consider what your contribution should be, and then use your skills and techniques to accomplish the same. Very often a manager tends to emphasize the sophistication of his job skills and techniques, losing sight of what his contribution to the organization ought to be. This causes organizational conflicts.

A successful manager attempts to resolve conflicting objectives by emphasizing contribution and smoothing out the differences between them.

> Roger D., the production manager of one of the world's leading straight stitch sewing machine factories, was a zealous protector and promoter of his department's needs and importance. He had set a deadline for getting the marketing department requirements every month for incorporation in the production program. His emphasis on production run efficiencies was so great that he avoided executing any urgent export or domestic orders received after the deadline. This resulted in the annoyance of a number of foreign and domestic customers and the loss of some orders.
>
> When Roger was reproached for not meeting such urgent orders, he would justify his actions on grounds of production efficiency considerations and technical limitations. All this resulted in

restricting meaningful discussions between the men in the field marketing and production departments. Roger D. felt that he was doing his job very well and achieving his managerial objectives. Despite objections to his approach, voiced by the field marketing staff, he found consolation in furthering what he felt were the objectives of the production function. Roger D. anticipated and looked forward to becoming the general manager, due to his long service with the company. However, top management realized he would never be able to relate to overall company objectives and bring his and the company's goals into congruence.

Very often, managers such as Roger are unsuccessful in reaching the positions they hope to attain. Sometimes such managers even lose their jobs, to be replaced by others who give priority to the overall organizational objectives and also take steps to safeguard their departmental interests.

In this case, Roger retired early. He was replaced by Stan B., a production manager with an impressive success record. On taking over his new job, Stan soon realized the department's need to accommodate rush orders, especially those that clearly benefitted the company despite the additional set-up and tooling costs. Stan started accepting such rush orders, and on a mutually agreed system, debited the marketing department with the extra costs of meeting these orders. This enabled the new production manager to keep within the budgeted production department costs. The marketing department was satisfied, as the increased sales turnover more than adequately justified such debits. Soon the company's profits showed a sharp increase. The new production manager made this possible by bringing his own department's objectives in line with the overall organizational objectives of economic performance. Top management regarded this manager as one of their most liked and efficient managers, and promoted him to the specially created position of associate general manager, at a salary of $50,000 a year.

Thus, by focussing on contribution rather than performance, a manager can smooth out differences in conflicting objectives.

HOW TO ACHIEVE YOUR PERSONAL OBJECTIVES

Your personal objectives can best be achieved if they are realistically based on performance in the organizational context. Therefore, the first step for you, the manager, is to see that your personal objectives are not in any sense contradictory or opposed to the organizational objectives. Once your objectives are brought into conformity with organizational objectives, you should set clear and definite goals which you want to achieve in the long run as well as in the short run. Then you can use this effectiveness in managing people to successfully achieve these goals.

Chapter 2

HOW TO DEAL WITH
WHAT OTHER PEOPLE WANT

In the process of managing people you have to deal repeatedly with what other people want. Thus, as a manager, your effectiveness and success in dealing with your people depends upon how well you are able to understand their needs and motivate them. This is the basis of minimizing conflict and stress in any group.

It is also important when dealing with people to understand and be able to control the impact of informal "cliques." In some cases, the authority of the "clique" may equal or exceed your own. Understanding the extent and source of your managerial authority is an important requirement for being effective.

In the following pages we shall discuss these topics in order to establish a successful pattern for dealing with people at different levels in the organization.

UNDERSTANDING COMMON HUMAN NEEDS

A group of men were trapped in a mine. After preliminary and cautious excavations, a narrow passage was created whereby air could reach them. This passage could not be increased due to the danger of the entire mine shaft collapsing. After having been in the mine for over two days, the men's first concern became food. They started clamoring for food. When it did not become possible to send them food for another two days, their shrieks and pleas for food could be heard via the flimsy air passage. A thin pipe was inserted through the path of the air passage whereby juice could be delivered to the famished men. Being assured that both air and food were possible, the men then became really concerned about their safety. There were pleas to get them out as soon as possible and to be careful that in the process of excavation they would not be buried alive. They were reassured with loudspeakers aimed through the air tunnel that special equipment was on its way and that they would be rescued shortly. As soon as the rescue operations were proceeding satisfactorily, and there was no doubt left that the men would be saved, they became exhilarated. Their next concern turned to whether there were newspapermen on hand to record their survival and the tremendous trauma they had been through. When they came to the surface, they were very much photographed and interviewed. In a final gesture of demands, they met the General Manager of the mines to request that they be given alternate work in the manufacturing facility of the same organization.

The example above illustrates what Maslow termed as the hierarchy of human needs. Initially, food became the most important concern. Maslow considers physiological drives as the most fundamental cause for the motivation of behavior. The hard fact of the matter is that physiological drives for food and sustenance are essential to the very maintenance of life. Thus, Maslow considers them as the most fundamental cause for the motivation of behavior. Fortunately, as these physiological needs are met, new needs of safety, love, power, etc. emerge to motivate people. Thus, we see man as a "wanting being" striving to satisfy many different needs. According to Maslow, these needs can be expressed as a hierarchy, with their order of potency as follows:

1. Physiological (Need for Nourishment)
2. Safety (Need for an orderly, familiar and predictable life)
3. Love (Need for affection and belonging)
4. Esteem (Need for self-respect and the esteem of others)
5. Self-actualization (Need to do and be what corresponds to an individual's inherent capabilities)

You will find that most people have all these drives to some extent. However, their order and the motivational pull of each need differs with time and the situation. Do all individuals among the people in your department have the same needs? Clearly, they don't. Even though physiological, safety, love, etc. need structures (in a particular subculture and culture) tend to be similar, they still vary with individuals because each individual has a unique personality. In this context, you can look at any individual personality in relation to the particular order and strength of each need, for physiological nourishment, safety, love, esteem, ' or self-actualization. Thus, an artist may place self-actualization, in terms of creativity, high on *his* hierarchy of needs; that is, this need must be satisfied before he thinks of esteem, status or power.

You may consider other types of human needs to be more "basic." Other observers have related needs such as sex, altruism, etc. to the basic five-need level model of Maslow. Thus, you can look upon sex as a vehicle for need satisfaction, ranging from simple physiological drives to aspirations for affiliation and power. Similarly, altruism may be an ego drive reflecting needs for affection and achievement.[1]

Obviously, the order of people's needs may vary under different circumstances. Despite its limitations, the concept of the "need hierarchy" is useful for the manager. You will discover that, as lower level needs of your people are relatively satisfied, they become less effective as motivators. An individual is motivated mainly by the next upper level of unsatisfied need. Gratified needs in a sense disappear. A hungry person may work hard for food and once fed, he will no longer work for food. Once a need is fully met it is not motivating. However, an individual may have his needs at different levels only partially met. In such a case, all such needs will motivate this individual in proportion to the unmet level of each need.

As a manager, you can attempt to influence the human behavior of your work group by considering what needs are relatively unsatisfied. You may find people in your work group seem to need status, respect, affection or self-actualization. These can then serve as levers for motivating the individuals concerned. Many managers neglect to meet the *unfulfilled higher level needs* of their employees. The traditional management tendency has been to emphasize financial incentives. As long as the workers severely need money, it works as a motivator. This incentive, however, can only partially satisfy the esteem and recognition needs of individuals.

---

[1] For a further review of the need hierarchy see A.H. Maslow's, "A Theory of Human Motivation: The Basic Needs" in David R. Hampton, Charles E. Summer, Ross A. Webber, *Organizational Behavior and the Practice of Management,* Scott, Foresman and Co., Illinois, 1968, pp. 27-40.

Therefore, it is often more effective for you, as a manager, to motivate your employees through measures such as bestowing your confidence and trust on the deserving; providing a system for continuously recognizing good individual and group performance; introducing flexibility in work allocation and assignments to utilize the best abilities of your group members, etc. These satisfy the affiliation, esteem and to some extent, the self-actualization needs of employees, which can be much more motivating than the lure of more money once a worker is earning enough to adequately provide for such lower level needs as food and shelter.

Beyond a certain income level, the motivation to work hard provided through opportunities for group affiliation and recognition (love and esteem needs) tends to be much more effective than the attraction of further monetary gain.

The famous experiments at the Hawthorne plant of Western Electric around 1920 demonstrated that money, as an incentive resulting from production bonuses, quotas, etc. motivates individual employees only up to a certain degree. Scientific experimenters observed a steep rise in the productivity of the employees who were consciously being studied in the Hawthorne experiments, regardless of the experimental conditions. Why were they suddenly so productive? Such employees felt they were part of a "special group of people" and, being aware that their performance was being recognized, they happily produced much more than they had in the past. When the work studies were analyzed in depth, the observers found that the production incentives did not motivate the workers to produce to their full capacity, whereas opportunities for group affiliation and recognition strongly motivated them to bring about a sharp rise in productivity.

You, as a practicing manager, can benefit greatly by recognizing the necessity of non-financial motivators to meet the "higher needs" of employees.

UNDERSTANDING EMPLOYEE MOTIVATION

Let us see how work is related to meeting the various needs of individuals, and how you can motivate them in an organizational environment.

Obviously, a job is directly related to obtaining physiological necessities and satifying safety and security needs. But what of the next higher levels on the need hierarchy? Does an ordinary job have any relationship to a person's social needs for affiliation, membership, affection and love? Recent experience has shown that it certainly does.

One of the interesting findings of the Hawthorne plant studies was that many workers limited their personal effort in order to maintain their membership in an informal social structure. They did not want to "outshine" their friends, even to earn a production bonus. To them, the desire for communications, support and friendship with associates on the job became more important than the little bit of extra money that might be earned.

A job provides two ways of satisfying the affiliation needs of an individual: first, by providing for the maintenance of a family, and second, by establishing social relations with fellow employees. Thus, social relationships and informal groups can be work motivators if they satisfy the affiliation needs of different employees. If, as a manager, you foster and encourage this, it will aid the employee commitment and performance of your group.

A job can also provide social esteem, status or prestige. Within an organization, the hierarchies of positions, their status symbols and perquisites reflect the desire for status differentiation. A manager should, therefore, always co-relate the title, pay, authority and status symbols amongst his subordinates as far as practical.

A large insurance company's regional office was set up for maximum space economy. Clerks, secretaries, representatives, supervisors, claim men and department heads were all seated at similar desks, row after row. Thomas McK., the regional manager, was having difficulty with superior-subordinate relations, particularly with supervisory morale. Though the more senior and able employees had suitable titles and got more money, they were dissatisfied. Mr. McK. discovered that the principal cause of dissatisfaction was the lack of *physical manifestation* of status differences, and he decided to introduce the required status differences. He provided individual offices to give quiet and privacy to the department heads. The supervisors were given additional facilities to make their working conditions efficient and more dignified. This had a tremendous impact on improving the supervisory morale and *improving* superior-subordinate relations.

Employees can also derive the satisfaction of "self-actualization" needs from their jobs when jobs are designed around individuals, rather than individuals fitted to rigid job descriptions. Perhaps the term "self-actualization" is too ambiguous in characterizing an important higher need of employees. Therefore, some managers and psychologists have identified three higher needs within "self-actualization"—needs for competence, power and achievement.

Undoubtedly, a major contribution to self-esteem can come from competent performance of one's job. In fact, the drive for self-esteem and competence is the instinct for good *workmanship*—a human characteristic untapped by most managers. Most men want to feel that they are doing something *important*. Individuals want to feel that they are contributing members of society. There is satisfaction derived from the dependence and gratitude of others.

Even so, the drive for competence is mainly internal. You will often notice that as a man obtains some social esteem he shifts from being "other-directed" and becomes more "inner-directed" in an effort to further satisfy himself. He cares less about what others think of his work, more about what *he* thinks. Thus, successful employees tend to become more individualistic and resist managerial conformity. As long as the manager can keep the "competence drive" of such employees going in a positive manner, he will get good performance. Such employees show a high "achievement need."

Both power and achievement needs are characteristic drives to exceptional performance. The achievement need is manifest in efforts to meet standards of excellence. The high achiever has a basic attitude towards life—when challenged, he tries harder and demands more of himself. Therefore, he accomplishes more. The achievement oriented person does not disregard tangible rewards, but he does not regard them as essential. He takes a special joy in winning or in competing successfully with a tough standard. In general, individuals with a high level of achievement motivation are more consistent, realistic and action-minded than individuals with other kinds of motivational patterns. Low achievers, on the other hand, will not project any optimism or positive imagination.

As a manager, you can attempt to estimate and evaluate the achievement drive within different employees. Those employees that demonstrate high achievement drives should be given greater responsibilities and the opportunity to meet performance targets. In fact, the need for achievement may be the most important factor in employee success.

MOTIVATION AT WORK

The late Douglas MacGregor was the first to point out that managers too often assume that employees view work as punishment. Therefore, they tend to motivate employees through external controls and threats of punishments in terms of the job. He called these his "Theory X" assumptions. The "carrot and stick" means of motivation which goes along with Theory X works reasonably well under certain conditions. Willingness to hire, high wages, and promises of promotion serve as "carrots"—threats of firing, suspensions without pay, etc. are "sticks." To a certain degree, the means of satisfying an employee's physiological and safety needs can be provided or withheld by the manager. Employment, wages, working conditions and benefits are such means. By these means you, as a manager, can control an individual under you as long as he is struggling for subsistence.

But the "carrot and stick" approach does not work at all once an employee has reached an adequate subsistence level and is motivated primarily by higher needs. You cannot provide your employee with self-respect or with the respect of his fellows, or with the satisfaction of needs for self-fulfillment. You can only create conditions so that the employee is encouraged and enabled to seek such satisfactions for himself. These conditions can be created when the "Theory Y" assumptions of MacGregor are applied. These assumptions recognize that employees do not inherently dislike work since work is a natural phenomenon, just as play or rest. Furthermore, as contrasted with Theory X, the following additional five assumptions are made:

1. Control and threat of punishment are not the only means of generating efforts toward organizational objectives. An employee will largely self-direct and self-control himself in the service of objectives *to which he is committed.*

2. The greater the *significance* of the rewards, the greater the commitment of employees to objectives. Amongst the more significant rewards are the satisfaction of ego and self-actualization needs.

3. The average employee, under proper conditions, will not only accept but seek responsibility.

4. Imagination and creativity for solving organizational problems is widely spread amongst the employees of an

organization. The more the manager applies the concept of "participative management," the more he can utilize the resources available in his employees. [2]

5. In the existing working environment, generally, the potential abilities of the average employee are only partially utilized.

Does this mean that under Theory Y, you, as a manager, have no control over your people? These assumptions of Theory Y [3] by no means imply that the removal of all control is a necessary, workable alternative to Theory X authoritarianism. They do indicate, however, the possibility of human growth and development, and stress adaptiveness rather than a single absolute form of control. They do point toward the possibility and advantages of employee involvement, under favorable conditions, [4] in the setting and implementation of objectives. As a manager, your understanding and application of Theory Y assumptions will not only equip you to deal with what other people's needs are, but will also enable you to motivate them effectively.

It is important at this stage for you to clearly distinguish between different needs and their motivation in the work environment. Frederick Herzberg, as research director of the Psychological Service of Pittsburgh, conducted an elaborate study of accounting and engineering personnel to determine the factors that satisfy and those that dissatisfy employees. [5] He reported that employees in both groups cited factors inherent in performing work as satisfying and factors surrounding work as dissatisfying. Thus *achievement, recognition,* and *work itself* are satisfiers. Working *conditions,* company *policy* and administration and interpersonal relations are *dissatisfiers.* Herzberg reports that an increase in the "satisfiers" is associated with improving performance on the job.

For this reason he calls the satisfiers "motivators." The environment *dissatisfiers* are termed by him as "hygiene factors" in

---

[2] For an application of this approach to examples of actual situations, please see Chapter 10.

[3] The well known Theory X and Theory Y assumptions discussed here have been expounded by Douglas MacGregor in *The Human Side of Enterprise,* published by McGraw Hill, 1960, pp. 33-48.

[4] These conditions have been discussed in Chapter 10 under "Involvement and Participation."

[5] Those interested in the technical details of the study please see Herzberg, Frederick, *Work and the Nature of Man,* World, 1966.

the sense implied in preventive medicine. In other words, an increase in the dissatisfiers prevents dissatisfaction but does not mean more motivation (just as hygiene may help prevent infection but does not inherently mean more health). The primary implication of Herzberg's work for the manager is that improving working conditions, establishing good policies and improving interpersonal relations in his group are good only in so far that dissatisfaction is minimized. But to motivate the people in his group, he needs to design jobs and allocate work so as to yield higher level need satisfaction to the employees in his groups.

Overemphasis on improving the "hygiene factors" for a group of employees *will not* give the motivational effect which a manager may be anticipating. To really motivate employees, the manager has to create the conditions whereby employees can get opportunities through their jobs to satisfy their achievement, recognition and other higher level needs. Improvements in the "hygiene factors" are most beneficial when the "motivators" or "job expectation" factors are satisfactory.

The "motivators" or "job expectation" factors do differ amongst employees. Generally, however, every employee would fall into one of the following three categories:

1. *An employee with a truncated need structure:* Such an employee is influenced only by the lower level needs, and therefore will be motivated to obtain only money or minimum social satisfaction through his job (friendships with co-workers). It is irrelevant whether the job or the manager offers opportunities for competence, power or achievement. In fact, these opportunities may confuse and upset such an employee, particularly if the manager attempts to appeal to the satisfaction of any higher-level needs. As a manager, your effectiveness with such an employee will depend upon how well you exercise your authority over the means to satisfy the lower needs, such as pay, working conditions, working hours, etc.

2. *An employee with developed higher needs which he pursues away from his job:* Such a person has been taught or believes that a job is an "unpleasant necessity," and work a "punishment." He will therefore be motivated to obtain only money and minimum social satisfaction on the job, and to use the money to satisfy higher needs (through hobby or church groups, athletics, etc.). It is

irrelevant whether the job or the manager offers opportunities for competence, power or achievement. As a manager, your effectiveness will depend upon how well you exercise your authority over the means to satisfy his lower needs.

3. *An employee with developed higher needs which he pursues on the job:* Such an individual believes that a job can provide opportunities for competence, power and achievement. If the job or the manager does not offer these opportunities, the employee will probably retaliate with behavior detrimental to himself as well as to the organization. On the other hand, if you, as a manager, provide him with opportunities for the fulfillment of these higher needs, he will be immensely motivated, and will generate behavior constructive to both himself and the organization.

As a manager, you can estimate what the needs of each of your employees are on the basis of the above categorization. By doing this you will be able to deal with their wants more effectively, and thereby motivate them toward better performance on the job.

MINIMIZING CONFLICT AND STRESS IN YOUR GROUP

In addition to the need for motivating employees, a manager is often faced with a situation of dysfunctional stress and conflict in his work group.

What causes stress and conflict in a work group? There are generally two major reasons. The first is interpersonal conflict. Managers often blame this on personality problems or the incompetence of individuals. It is not uncommon to find two employees in a work group who can't get along with each other, or an employee who has difficulty in cooperating with anyone. While it is true that some people cause stress and conflict by their nature and mannerisms, the more common reason for interpersonal conflict is frustration. This arises when an internal barrier stands between a motivated employee and his goals. When the barrier is not overcome, or when the motivation to do something which the barrier is obstructing becomes stronger, then a number of responses may result. In the work situation, the barrier may be attacked symbolically (e.g., throwing darts at a picture of the boss) or organizationally (by "work slowdown," "forgetting," or "sabotage"). Although frustration is the major cause for aggression, it may also occur from an employee's power motives and a certain love for conflict.

Although, as mentioned above, people are sometimes the source of conflict and stress in the group, the second and more prevalent cause arises from faulty communication flows in the organization. Unfortunately, this is often overlooked by the practicing manager, resulting in continuing stress and conflict in his work group. Organization structure is the formal design of work flow, and largely determines the flow of interactions in the organization—who initiates and who responds, who sees whom, how often, etc. When these structurally determined communication patterns conflict with employee personality patterns, stress is produced. This stress can be minimized only through a change in behavior.

Ernie T., an experienced manager, was transferred to a new department, but continued to spend his accustomed amount of time with his subordinates. His new position, however, required that Ernie frequently meet and consult with his fellow department heads. When he neglected to do this because of his habitual preoccupation with his departmental work, other departmental heads started pressuring him. As the new pressures built up, Ernie was quick to realize that he must modify his interactional pattern to reduce tension and dissatisfaction, or his organizational position would be threatened. He therefore began to devote more time to working with his fellow department heads.

There are three interaction patterns in the organization which cause detrimental stress:

1. Uni-flow interaction
2. Insufficient and irregular interaction
3. Changing and unpredictable interaction

Uni-flow interaction

Every employee resents always *receiving* communications and having to respond to his bosses, with no opportunity to initiate communications. Furthermore, if the one-way initiation often contains criticism, the feelings of stress are obviously heightened. Therefore, as a manager, you have to see that opportunities for two-way communication are provided in your working group.

Insufficient interaction

Any working relationship in which the interactional flow bet-

ween individuals is fragmented and infrequent tends to generate
stress and conflict. This is illustrated by the following example.

> The sales department of a large engineering factory making
> castings, tools and sewing machine components was divided into
> four sections—export, in-country distribution, claims and
> replacement, and shipping. It was a "sales-service" department, as
> the actual selling function was handled by the field sales
> organization. The work flow in the department was such that there
> was only intermittent interaction between the supervisor, Boyd G.,
> of the claims and replacement section, and Marvin R., supervisor of
> the shipping section. These supervisors could not get along with
> each other, and each one was quick to blame the other whenever a
> claim for replacement had to be processed. Kent S., the sales
> manager, thought this trouble was a problem of the two strong and
> conflicting personalities involved, since Boyd and Marvin got along
> very well with the rest of the department staff. Kent decided to
> redistribute the work load in his department by promoting the
> supervisor of the in-country distribution section out into the field
> sales organization. He then made Boyd supervisor of a combined in-
> country distribution, claims and replacement section. Boyd was a
> well qualified supervisor. The only thing which worried Kent was
> whether Boyd would be able to improve his working relationship
> with the supervisor of the shipping section, Marvin. However, the
> changed work flow in the department brought these two supervisors
> into regular contact everyday. This resulted in their developing a
> mutual trust and reliability within a few weeks, and practically
> removed their earlier stressful conflicts.

Inadequate interaction does not give an opportunity for individuals to develop mutual trust and understanding. This is one of
the reasons why the staff and line groups generate conflict and
stress in each other. The interaction between them tends to be
intermittent, which doesn't help to remove mutual doubts of each
other's authority and capability. As a manager, you can help to
minimize stress and conflict under conditions of inadequate interaction. Here's what to do:

1. Redesign the work allocations to give opportunities for greater
work oriented interaction between employees.

2. Encourage social interaction through group activities outside
the work environment, without letting it become too demanding.
There is widespread agreement that an adequate amount of social

interaction is essential to keep stress and conflict at a minimum within a working group.

Thus, as a manager, you have to be aware that inadequacy both in work communications and social interaction can be stressful in a work group.

Changing interaction

Employees do not like adjusting to unexpected changes in initiation and response patterns. In any working situation over a period of time, people become familiar with each other's working habits, approach to problems, type of suggestions each would automatically accept or reject, etc. Frequent transfers of personnel should therefore be avoided, as they upset these relationships and require the building up a new relationship between different employees from scratch.

Changes in procedures, policy, technology, etc., also modify interactional patterns. When these changes are introduced unilaterally without consultation and apparent justification, they tend to generate stress and conflict in the work environment. An example of how dramatically a simple procedural change can affect interactional patterns is illustrated below.

Stan DeH., manager of a development department, was concerned about the low productivity of his department. His engineers often complained about the time they had to spend assisting sales people to solve quotational problems. The salesmen individually consulted the development engineers whenever they felt it was necessary. Stan issued a departmental order that all salesmen would have to record their times in and out of the development department by making an entry in a register. Obviously, the purpose of the register was to measure the amount of time the salesmen spent in the development department.

The very first sales executive to enter the development department after the order had been issued was advised to sign the register. The sales executive ignored this advice and went on ahead to the engineer he wanted to see. However, the engineer refused to discuss anything unless the sales executive signed the register. An argument started, ending up in the sales executive stomping away with indignation. The development manager then went to see the marketing manager, and demanded that all sales personnel sign the register. This resulted in all the sales personnel agreeing to sign the register when ordered by their superior. Actually, however, many of them ceased consulting the development department. Communication flow between the two departments was drastically reduced. The company objectives obviously suffered because the sales personnel stopped quoting on products requiring engineering assistance in order to avoid the development department as much as possible. The sales personnel were not so much against having their visits recorded as they were against the manner in which change was introduced. They felt that the development department assistant or secretary could record visits in the register, if it was so important. Furthermore, if they or their manager had been consulted prior to the change, then things would have been different and they would have cooperated.

The above incident shows how a simple but sudden change in communication patterns, when improperly introduced, can generate extreme stress and conflict. A manager, therefore, has to see that a change in interaction patterns, whenever necessary, is introduced after necessary consultation and discussion with those who are going to be affected by the change.[6]

As a manager, you can take the following approaches to minimize conflict and stress in your group.

1. *Work allocation:* When necessary, adjust work allocation to reorient conflicting personalities. Motivate desirable organization behavior, such as cooperation at the time of reorientation.[7]

2. *Interaction and Communication:* Check that communication flow in the group is not uni-directional, insufficient or subject to sudden change. If so, then reorient communication patterns and work allocations so that communications become two way or multidirectional, regular, adequate and predictable. Also encourage social interaction to supplement work related interaction.

3. *Group cohesiveness:* Increase group cohesiveness through such measures as free and informal communications, stable membership, common values and standards, mutual dependency and individual participation in group objective setting and implementation.

---

[6] The crucial aspect of how the manager can introduce and manage change, without generating undue stress and resistance, is discussed in Chapter 10.

[7] In this regard, please also review Chapter 12, which deals with how to manage problem people.

4. *Coordination of bargains:* Competition and conflict will tend to appear in any working group because of the basic political nature of man. Organizational decisions are often made on the basis of bargaining powers of those whose views and interests clash. Because of the complexity of these internal bargaining processes and their danger to organizational effectiveness, you, as a manager, have to take the responsibility to coordinate and mediate amongst the conflicting interests which may be present in your group. In doing so you may be able to fruitfully employ one of the three approaches mentioned above.

Generally, managers tend to treat conflict and stress in the group as having to do primarily with personality problems. They neglect to consider other causes such as faulty communication flows, group disintegrative tendencies, faulty work allocations and lack of coordination of different pressure groups. As a manager, you can minimize stress and conflict in your group by following the four approaches mentioned above.

CONTROLLING THE IMPACT OF INFORMAL CLIQUES

In dealing with what other people want, as a manager it will be to your advantage to know about and understand the informal groups within your organization. Only by doing so will you be in a position to control their impact.

As man is basically a social animal, the informal construction and extension of organization is common human practice. It is a primary fact that man lives in groups with other people. It has been somewhat traditional, however, to view informal cliques or groups in the organization as being essentially detrimental to it. It has been demonstrated in recent studies and experiences with informal groups that they can aid and further organizational objectives to a tremendous degree. The impact and importance of the informal organization has been dramatically brought out in a study done to determine the great contrast which existed between the behavior of the prisoners of war during the Second World War and the Korean War in 1950.

Jubilation and happiness characterized the American prisoners freed from Nazi Germany, whereas sullenness and enmity was typical of those freed in Korea. Investigation indicated differences in the organization and treatment of the prisoners in Nazi Germany and communist Korea. In the Nazi camps, the prisoners were dealt with through a military structure. The imprisoned officers were required to police and maintain the internal organization. After interrogation, the prisoners were returned to the same group, the expectation being that the unfortunate, tortured men would serve as examples to frighten others into talking. Despite the mistreatment, bad food and clothing, there was a relatively low death rate, many escapes and hardly any instances of collaboration. The conditions in Korea were different. The prisoners did not receive any worse food or clothing than their guards. In prison camps, officers were separated from enlisted men, and sometimes lower ranking men were intentionally placed in charge of noncommissioned officers to disrupt both formal and informal acceptance of leadership. Prisoners were periodically transferred, and groups systematically broken up to avoid the development of a military or informal organization amongst the prisoners.

Except in a few extreme cases, the Koreans generally used relatively little physical torture. After a prisoner was interrogated, he would appear elsewhere in camp, seemingly well, and usually with new clothes. This meant that the prisoners did not know what to expect, and they could not brace themselves psychologically. Furthermore, this created distrust and suspicion over the behavior of friends. All this created low morale, high death rate, few escapes, general ill health and instances of compromising answers.

The above example brings out the impact which an informal organization can have on group morale, tenacity and performance. Morale is a group activity, and people must get organized both formally and informally to carry out group objectives.

What does an informal clique or group really offer to an employee? It offers three things as brought out in the above example.

1. *The fulfillment of social needs.* Practical experience amongst work groups indicates that employees who have no opportunity for social contact find their work unsatisfying. This may reflect itself in low production, absenteeism and high employee turnover. Elton Mayo, in as early as 1946, observed that the employees of a textile plant who worked in isolated jobs were dissatisfied and failed to meet production standards. When the textile company permitted such employees to take rest periods as a group, both satisfaction and production increased.[8] This is as true today as it ever was in

---

8 For details of the study please see Mayo, E., *The Human Problems of an Industrial Civilization.* Graduate School of Business Administration, Harvard University, 1946.

the past. Hospitals have discovered that maids feel uncomfortable when they work only in the company of doctors and nurses. However, when three or four of them are grouped together as a team, turnover is reduced and a more efficient job is done. It has been found that the enjoyment and assistance derived from information associations on the job helps to make it more pleasant, and thereby more productive.

2. *Identification and emotional support.* Self-image is derived from social image. In the office or on the shop floor, the informal group can guide the individual in knowing what is desirable and undesirable behavior. Even where established rules exist, a question always remains about the extent to which everyone is expected to live by the letter of the law. How much time should one take for a coffee break? What papers need to be marked to the general manager? Do all copy need to be shown to the advertising manager? What is the best time to get sanctions on important work orders from the boss? The informal and formal groups both provide guidelines to employees as to organizational behavior, desirable in terms of not only written policies but also in terms of what is actually acceptable.

The emotional support, which both a formal and informal group identification provides, encourages people to excell in order to bring a good name to the group. The manager therefore need not be afraid of informal group formation. If approached positively, it can serve to identify the employee with desirable and acceptable organizational performance and provide him the emotional support to be consistently productive.

3. *Assistance in meeting goals.* Groups, both formal and particularly informal, tend to assist their individual members in solving specific problems. It has been found that employees tend to turn to their fellow employees for help first, as opposed to going to their manager. When the informal groups have goals in harmony with the organization's needs, then they aid the achievement of managerial objectives.

The informal groups are generally related to the formal organization and are affected by the technological aspects of work flow. Informal groups are composed of employees who (1) frequently communicate with each other on the job and (2) have similar likes and dislikes.

As a manager, you will have to deal with informal cliques simply because they always emerge from the formal organization.

Therefore, you cannot treat your employees only as individuals without considering the impact of informal groups amongst them. It is particularly important to understand the relationship between formal and informal status systems and to try and maintain continuity between them. Thus, an employee who is informally recognized as being the leader of the informal group should be groomed into formal leadership. It would be inviting trouble to disregard such informal leadership amongst employees and appoint people on other considerations from within the group into leadership or supervisory positions. If such employees are not acceptable as being deserving in the informal group, then they will not get the respect or cooperation necessary for them to be effective organizationally.

As a manager, therefore, it is certainly advantageous to recognize and accept the assistance of informal groups. It would even be to your advantage to encourage their formation where the nature of individual jobs would not foster such formation. A manager can influence these groups positively through:

1. His leadership.
2. Changing or redesigning work-flow patterns and organizational structure,
3. Using the principles of managing change [9] and
4. By sensitivity training to improve relationships. [10]

A manager stands to benefit by recognizing and accepting informal groups as an essential part of any organization and controlling their impact as discussed, so that they serve to meet both employee and organizational needs.

THE SOURCE OF YOUR MANAGERIAL AUTHORITY

In dealing with the needs of your employees and those of the formal and informal groups which exist in the organization, it is beneficial to keep in mind the source of your managerial authority.

The obvious source is the position in the organization vested in you by the organization through its top management. This position gives you the power of rewarding and punishing employees, which

[9] This is discussed in Chapter 10.

[10] For a discussion on how to use this technique, please see Chapter 11.

induces them to obey you. Other sources of your authority are your own personal charisma, leadership traits and the socio-cultural deference arising from your experience and social status. But perhaps the least understandable and one of the most important sources of your authority is the acceptance afforded to you by your subordinates. As long as your communications are objectively based on better and more complete information (as is usually the case), there will be a cooperative personal attitude amongst the individuals working under you. Thus, for your authority to be truly effective, you need to be the center of the system of communication in your organization group, and there needs to be an attitude of personal cooperation amongst your employees. Both factors are interdependent on each other.

To strengthen your position of authority in a practical way, you would need to make sure that you get adequate information from the organizational structure, so that orders or instructions automatically have a high response of cooperation and acceptance by your employees. It is advantageous to review whether there is any information you are not getting upon which you need to base your decisions and instructions. If so, then arrange to get this information to further increase your credibility and acceptance amongst your own group. This will invariably enable you to deal with the needs of your people more effectively.

With respect to authority, employees can be categorized into three kinds.

1. Those who have a feeling of comfort in having others as leaders and in following all rules and regulations. Such employees may be categorized as "dependents."

2. Those who derive feelings of discomfort towards other people in authority and to following rules and regulations. Such employees may be categorized as "counter dependents."

3. Those who have no preconceived feelings for or against people in authority and rules and regulations. They measure each situation and manager without stereotyping them, i.e., objectively. Such employees may be categorized as "independents."

If an employee falls in either of the first two groups he will tend to alternate between the extremes of submission and rebellion. Consider the case of an employee who views all superiors as being helpful. As this is not the case in reality, he will cling to this view on the surface, but will have an underlying distrust of all superiors.

Therefore, he will tend to move within the extremes of submission and rebellion. The same is true of the employee who believes that all authority systems are bad. Since in reality there are some good leaders, he would also let his attitude vary between rebellion and submissiveness. Employees who fall in the third category are the most productive, as their attitudes are not preconceived and therefore do not vary in the unrealistic and undesirable range of complete submissiveness and rebellion. On the other hand, their attitude is realistic in terms of particular situations, which provides for greater understanding and cooperation from them in the work environment.

As a manager, you would benefit by making your employees who fall in the first two categories discover the need to change their preconceived notions. This can be achieved by discussing the matter individually and proposing what the employees' approach should be. A more effective method is the use of sensitivity training, which is discussed in Chapter 11.

As a manager, your ability to strengthen your sources of authority, as well as to categorize and improve the attitudes of your people towards authority systems, will assist you in dealing with their needs with greater credibility and better results.

ESTABLISHING YOUR PATTERN FOR DEALING WITH EMPLOYERS

How can you be "democratic" in your relations with subordinates while maintaining the necessary authority and control in the organization? This is a problem faced by all modern managers.

The answer can not be a rigid one, as it would need to be relevant to various situations and needs. A good pattern of behavior for a manager in dealing with his subordinates is to use different leadership styles to suit different situations. To be more specific, let us first see what the different leadership patterns are that a manager can use effectively.

Figure 1 presents a range of possible leadership behavior available to a manager.

At one extreme is the possibility of the manager himself identifying a problem, considering alternatives and choosing one of them for implementation by his subordinates. At the other extreme is the manager who sets general guidelines consistent with the

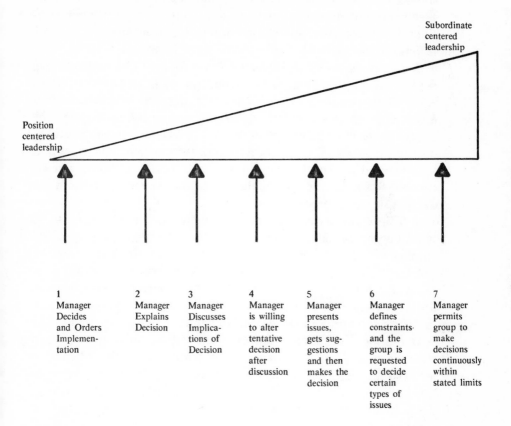

1	2	3	4	5	6	7
Manager Decides and Orders Implementation	Manager Explains Decision	Manager Discusses Implications of Decision	Manager is willing to alter tentative decision after discussion	Manager presents issues, gets suggestions and then makes the decision	Manager defines constraints and the group is requested to decide certain types of issues	Manager permits group to make decisions continuously within stated limits

Figure 1

organizational guidelines, and then turns the decisions over to the group, of which he may include himself as a member. Such a pattern is only occasionaly encountered, and is particularly effective for research development groups where the teams of engineers or managers identify and diagnose the problem, develop alternative solutions, and then decide on what appears to be the best course of action.

In a practical situation, how would the manager decide what type of leadership pattern he should use? This would depend upon three major considerations:

1. *The Manager's Value System and Personality.* The manager's own convictions and opinions regarding the share his subordinates

should have in decision-making would influence the end of the spectrum toward which he is inclined to operate. Other considerations would be his confidence in his subordinates and his feelings of security in dealing with uncertainty.

2. *The Nature and Behavior of Subordinates.* The manager can permit greater freedom to his subordinates if certain conditions exist. These conditions are discussed in detail in Chapter 10, but essentially center around the following prerequisite, viz., that the subordinates must be ready and willing to assume responsibility for decision-making. If, on the other hand, they have no desire for and have learned to expect authoritative directives, it would only cause concern to suddenly confront them with the request to share in the decision-making process.

3. *The Nature of the Situation.* The considerations here are the type of organization and its existing value systems, the ability of the employees to work effectively as a group and the nature of the problem. Employees may not have the necessary experience or information to make certain types of decisions. *The key question for the manager to always ask is whether he has heard everyone who has the necessary knowledge and experience to make a signficiant contribution.* Recent experiences of managerial effectiveness have shown that a fairly high degree of subordinate centered behavior leads to higher employee motivation, readiness of subordinates to accept change, improvement in the quality of managerial decisions, development of teamwork and the individual development of employees.

A successful leadership pattern is based on the three major considerations outlined above. It is, of course, not enough to perceive these considerations alone, but to behave appropriately, in the light of the total situation. Thus, if direction is in order, the manager is able to direct, but where considerable participative freedom is necessary, he is able to provide such participative leadership. It is important that the manager convey to his subordinates whatever leadership pattern he may be using. As an example, if you decide to make a certain decision, but your subordinate group gets the impression that you have delegated this authority, confusion and resentment are likely to follow. It is therefore highly important for a manager to be honest and clear in describing what authority he is retaining and what role he is asking his subordinates to carry out in solving a particular problem.

ESTABLISHING YOUR PATTERN FOR DEALING WITH SUPERIORS

It is, of course, obvious that organizational success partly depends upon the ability to deal effectively with one's superiors. Sometimes this is not easy, particularly when your boss has a strong personality, different likes and dislikes and a number of what you consider grave weaknesses, such as a short temper, inconsistency in approaching similar situations, etc.

How do you deal with such a boss? Your pattern of dealing with a "bad" boss as well as a "good" boss can be based around a cardinal principle in dealing with people.

Emphasize and benefit from people's strengths. List in your own mind what some of the strengths of your boss are. Then put accent on these strengths in your dealings with him. If he has an excellent technical knowledge, then benefit from that by emphasizing the solution of technical problems as an important area in your dealings with him. Spare him from suffering in the areas where he is weak by keeping such dealings to a minimum.

This will have two major advantages. (1) You will benefit by getting good decisions in the strong areas of your boss. (2) Your boss will feel more comfortable and think better of you as he will be able to communicate easily and without stress more often with you. This is because it is simple human nature for people to like those who support and share their strengths.

Everyone has strengths and weaknesses. It is a good idea to accentuate the strengths of your superiors and leave their weaknesses alone as far as possible. The pleasure in discussing the weaknesses of one's superiors with other employees is not without danger. Constructive criticisms and discussions on the request of the boss is the best opportunity to go over his strengths and weaknesses in a positive manner.

It is also in the interest of every manager to help his superiors move up in areas where they offer no direct competition to him. An upward movement in the organization does generally result in opening various opportunities and faster promotions which may not even be foreseen initially.

As a manager, your pattern of dealing with your superiors should practically reflect your support and appreciation of their strong areas, your ability to take care of other areas without bringing attention to your superiors' weaknesses in these areas, and your support of their movement up in the organization to appropriate positions. With this approach, your superiors will help you get the results you want.

Chapter 3

SETTING OBJECTIVES
IN YOUR GROUP

The problem of deciding how to set objectives[1] is faced by all managers. There is only one practical way of doing this: by determining what shall be measured in each area and what the yardstick of measurement will be.

As a manager, you are responsible for the contribution of your component to the large organizational unit above and eventually to the enterprise. This means that the goals of your job must be defined by the contribution which you have to make to the success of the larger unit, of which you are a part. As this contribution would be the result of each individual employee's efforts in your group, your goals would be realistic only if based on the committed performance of your employees. Thus, it is to your direct benefit to involve each of your group members in setting their individual goals, and thereby the overall feasible goals of the group.

STARTING YOUR MANAGEMENT PROCESS

Goal setting, and its review, is the initial and most important aspect of the management process. Before exploring goal setting in any detail, let us be clear in our own minds about what is implied by the management process.

---

[1] For sake of simplicity, and consistent with common usage, the words objectives and goals are used synonymously.

Planning, Organizing, Integrating and Measuring is the definition of managerial work which has been used by the General Electric Company. Integrating refers to the role of the manager as a motivator and coordinator of the group's activities. Measuring signifies control through comparison of actual versus planned results. "Management is basically problem solving" is another approach which has gained ground due to the recent work on logical problem analysis and decision making. Getting things done through others is another common and well accepted way of looking at managing.

The management process certainly covers all of the above aspects. Its key function, however, has been recognized as *processing information to obtain results through people.* This broad approach places the right emphasis on the manager as being the focal point of information flow and communication in his work group. As indicated earlier, this is what gives the manager authority and the decision making ability. At any one time the manager has or should have the greatest amount of information with respect to any pertinent organizational activity. He can then communicate this information and coordinate the activities of his group towards desired organizational performance.

All managers must deal with the following five categories of information processing and communication.

1. *Setting goals.* These are things which a manager wants to attain but hasn't yet determined how. Reduced costs, fewer rejects, higher productivity, larger share of the market, etc. are a few examples. The role played by subordinates in identifying goals and establishing implementation schedules has a very beneficial effect on their long run motivation and teamwork—more so than any other single factor over which a manager has control. The technique and consideration involved in getting the successful participation of employees in goal setting have been dealt with extensively in Chapter 10.

2. *Developing alternatives.* Once goals have been decided on, it becomes necessary to consider different ways of achieving them. Developing alternatives to achieving set goals is the creative phase of the management process. The practical approaches to making your employees more creative will be treated in the next chapter.

3. *Evaluating alternatives.* It is the manager's responsibility to evaluate the various alternatives and choose the optimum approach

to achieving a set objective. Make evaluation a team play as far as possible. It is your associates and subordinates who will ultimately implement the chosen alternative, so it is essential that they get the best possible understanding of it and support it from the very beginning.

4. *Planning, organizing, and controlling.* These represent the designed coordination of human and material resources for scheduled goal achievement. These aspects are covered in greater detail further on in this chapter.

5. *Analyzing deviations.* No matter how good the planning and control, deviations will always occur. The manager's problem solving ability comes into play here. He must determine the causes for any negative deviations, and re-establish goals and objectives to correct the shortcomings where they occur.

As can be seen from the above discussion, the goal setting phase is the crucial phase of the management process. Setting goals in your work group to achieve organizational objectives is clearly your most important responsibility as a manager.

How can a manager best set goals in his work group? What are the consequences of your goal setting methods for productivity and morale amongst your associates and subordinates? What is the relationship between individual goals and organizational goals?

A review of these elementary questions can assist individual managers to:

1. Better define goals
2. Get a deeper insight into the motivations of employees and
3. Develop techniques for building organizational effectiveness and loyalty.

While talking about goal setting, it is important to bear in mind that it is basic human nature for most people to believe and act on their own ideas, rather than the recommendation or command of others. There are, of course, wide individual and situational variations, particularly in different cultures. However, today, employees in all cultures have a tendency to resist unilateral commands and imposed decisions. In every culture it has been found that wherever practical and appropriate,[2] participation of

---

[2] See Chapter 10 for the conditions necessary under which employee participation can be successful.

employees in goal setting tends to motivate them to committed and improved performance. This is particularly true of employees from a racial minority or a developing culture as humane treatment and recognition has a much greater value to them because of its general social scarcity.

As a manager you need two procedural tools to effectively set goals in your work group. These are:

1. A means of obtaining the information that will give you the group's best thinking and earnest support.

2. A system for organizing the information obtained, for purposes of review as well as evaluation and formulation of specific working plans and controls.

These two procedural tools can be initiated by following a four step approach outlined below. This approach to establishing goals can be easily adapted to suit different situations.

Step 1. List things which you think your group should be able to achieve in an ideal situation.

Step 2. Categorize the list into two portions, the required and the desired, to match the requirements and resources of your organizational operation. All items which could be dispensed with altogether if priorities make the sacrifice necessary should be categorized under desired. Others would fall in the required category.

Step 3. Break the required and desired items into their time, place and quantity elements to be more definitive.

Step 4. Map out a set of operating goals by setting priorities in each of the required and desired categories. The priorities amongst required goals will be based on their urgency with respect to time. Some required goals will need to be achieved before others can be accomplished. The priorities amongst desired goals would depend upon your management judgment as to their organizational importance in terms of increasing profitability. Other considerations such as improving morale, reducing turnover, developing employees, etc. should be incorporated in conjunction with the above.

This four step process can help a manager to convert vague wishes into a set of workable, preferable goals at any level in any organizational activity.

Since a manager performs through people, his success depends upon the support of his people in the organizational activity. Therefore, there are tremendous gains to be made by your involving your subordinates at each stage of the four step goal setting process. The intent and means of involvement should match the information need at each stage. In other words, you should determine the procedure that would be the most efficient for obtaining and organizing the required information. This approach will help you decide the following types of questions which arise from time to time.

- Is it better to ask them to give their ideas in writing or orally?
- Should I meet them individually or in a group?
- Will I need a single session or a series of meetings to accomplish this?
- Should I listen to what they have to say first before presenting my own ideas or vice versa?

Let us see how a manager successfully involved his subordinates in the four step goal setting process:

John D., the manager of the marketing department of a large organization, had recently read about the benefits of employee involvement in the goal setting process. He decided to try this approach by reviewing and re-establishing his group's goals through the participation of all concerned employees. John D. did this in the following way:

Step 1. He got the whole team together, choosing a time in the morning when they would be fresh and relaxed. He saw to it that they would not be disturbed during the 3 hours of the meeting. He then explained what he wanted to do, and invited their participation and ideas as they reviewed and discussed different items. He then reviewed where the department stood with respect to performance and budget. A list of goals was then presented by him, to which he asked for additions and modifications based on the ideas and reactions of the group. Some goals were pointed out as being too high to achieve without additional support from inventory control. Others were felt easily achievable and, in fact, increased slightly. The inventory control problem was fully discussed by the group together for the first time, and a satisfactory scheduling arrangement was worked out to avoid periods of stockouts and high inventory. A number of useful suggestions emerged with regard to increasing marketing effectiveness. It was decided to start a competitive activity report to share successful strategies in replacing competitive equipment.

Step 2. The modified list of goals was then categorized into the required and desired ideas. Problems, operational limitations, top management constraints, etc. were fully discussed. Notes were made by John D. and his section heads on how some of the operational limitations could be reduced. After adequate discussion, a list of required and desired goals was arrived at with group consensus.

Step 3. John D. then subdivided the group into smaller groups and individuals to pin down those goals in terms of a time and quantity schedule by those best suited to make realistic projections. He then scheduled another group meeting after two weeks, so that the entire team could meet to correct oversights and finalize the details of the required and desired lists of goals.

Step 4. The full team met and reviewed the time and performance targets set by each task group for individual goals. A few priorities had to be adjusted for coordination purposes. John D. was impressed with most of the targets set by the employees—they were more rigid than he would have set himself. Obviously, the sense of participation had motivated most employees to project their capabilities to boost up their team and individual recognition. John made sure that the targets were realistic. Those that were not were scaled down by the group through discussion.

John D. was really impressed with what employee participation in goal setting had yielded. He had a better set of goals than he himself could have established, because of some of the excellent suggestions which came forth from some of the experienced and talented employees. He could see how he could organize his group better and improve control by what he learned in observing individual employees in the participative process. He also realized that this had sown the seeds of mutual understanding and teamwork amongst his group, which would mean less working friction and misunderstanding.

Having a good set of realistic goals, backed by the support and commitment of the group, is the payoff which a manager gets when he involves his subordinates in the process of goal setting. This is a crucial aspect in managing people successfully, and can be used to significant advantage by every manager.

The next logical step is to organize the group to accomplish the goals which have been set.

ORGANIZING FOR THE TASKS YOUR GROUP MUST ACCOMPLISH

The purpose of organizing is to form formal and informal

relationships among people in order to co-ordinate organizational activities and implement plans efficiently. An organizational structure may be very rigidly defined or be sketched in general outlines that leave room for overlap and variation.

The question which faces you as a manager is how rigidly must you define structure. Should you define each job and limits of authority and responsibility in detail, or should you set up only operating guidelines to get the tasks accomplished by your group? There can, of course, be no one standard solution. Moreover, there are certainly important considerations which can aid you to determine the most effective organization of the group to get tasks accomplished. In general, time urgency, large numbers of employees, low skill levels and inexperience require sharp delineation of responsibility, authority and specific job descriptions. It must be remembered that the definition of operating boundaries does not necessarily limit creativity and freedom. Instead, it can help to release creativity by clearly specifying the territory within which innovation is needed and wherein the individual feels his field of opportunity lies.

A manager must delegate responsibility and authority sufficiently so that parts of the tasks do not "fall between two chairs." It is a good idea to divide the group into sections or task forces, with their responsibilities clearly specified and their leaders or heads chosen or appointed, as the case may be. The test of an appropriate organization structure is when the following do *not* occur:

1. Confusion over job responsibilities.
2. Jobs that are done twice.
3. Work which is left unfinished.
4. Lack of cooperation.
5. Misunderstandings arising from faulty communications.
6. Excessive demands on the manager's time for employee and operational problems.

When any of the above occur regularly, then it is an indication that the organizational structure of the group needs to be corrected.

While organizing your group for accomplishing organizational tasks, the following key points must be followed to ensure a successful working organization.

1. The work or tasks must be so subdivided as to give each individual a feeling of real accomplishment and contribution to his

group on their completion. The individual pieces of work must therefore be sufficiently difficult to challenge the employees and yield feelings of achievement.

2. The units of work or assignments must be measurable and standards established.The measures and standards must be explicit and understood by both the individual and the manager.

3. Each individual should be given the opportunity to spend as much time doing work that he is adept in as far as possible. Utilization of special skills is a great motivator.

4. The work of each individual should be structured so as to permit individual achievement as well as a share in group activity.

5. The organizational structure should be designed considering both the work to be done, as well as the individuals available and the skills they possess. It pays to think about who will be doing each piece of work, and to consult the individual concerned to take into account his recommendations and concerns.

6. Though supervisory and managerial skill can enable individuals to be successful, their chances of success are enhanced if they are familiar with the work content of the position they supervise.

7. You must constantly review the need for changing the organizational structure of the group, but keep reorganizations to the minimum as much as possible. Whenever a reorganization is necessary, it should be discussed in the group and be supported by the individuals concerned.

The above guidelines and considerations can effectively assist you in organizing your group to accomplish various specific tasks.

HOW TO DELEGATE TASKS WHICH MUST BE DONE

Every manager has to continuously delegate duties to different members of his working group according to its organization and the individual capabilities of its members. Although it is a common and basic management activity, delegation continues to be misunderstood and inefficiently handled. A clear understanding of its essential aspects will be a valuable asset to managers and their organizational groups.

Delegation centers around three essential aspects—duties, authority and accountability. Every time a manager delegates work to an employee—say a president to the sales director or a production superintendent to an operator—he explicitly or implicitly assigns duties, grants authority and creates an obligation to complete the job or assignment. No delegation is complete without a clear understanding being conveyed by the manager about the duties, authority and accountability involved. Within these three critical areas the implications for the manager are as follows:

1. *Duties.* These should not be described in terms of functions alone, as is generally done. In other words, it is inefficient to merely describe the duties of an employee as either to run a capstan lathe, sell in a specific territory or measure distribution costs. *You should describe duties in terms of the results you want to achieve.* In the three examples given above, this would mean that you would specify an employee's duties as to turn on the capstan lathe a certain number of pieces per day according to specifications, or to sell a particular amount of different items and service existing customers in a specific territory, or to measure distribution costs for purposes of pricing, controlling costs and locating warehouses.

Defining duties in terms of accomplishment adds vitality to work situations, and offers means of achievement satisfaction to the individuals involved. Since jobs differ, such accomplishments may be stated in terms of short term or long term goals, or both. Particular situations may require only general and intangible declarations, rather than specific and immediately accomplishable ones. Whatever the situation, it is important that we phrase delegation of duties in terms of goals. A subordinate will thereby be able to have advance notice of the criteria on which his performance will be rated. This will motivate him as he knows what activities he must perform, and with what results, in order to achieve appreciation and esteem.

2. *Authority.* If an employee is assigned duties, it is obvious that his manager must give him all the necessary authority to carry them out. Assigning responsibilities does not imply assigning authority. Authority must be assigned clearly in terms of permissions or rights, e.g., authorizations to buy sundry items, accept orders from customers, audit account records, etc. Authority cannot be delegated in an unlimited sense. It must still be within company policy and follow established and authorized procedures. Furthermore, while delegating authority, you might need to reserve to yourself decisions on certain matters, and clearly specify the boundaries within which the subordinates should operate.

Because of these various qualifications on authority, when you delegate tasks and duties you must specify clearly, in writing, to all concerned the rights and sanctions associated with the assigned duties. This will go a long way in motivating employees to achieve the objectives and tasks set by you. It is important to bear in mind that recent trends in organizations all over the world have shown a reduction in the degree of authority which can be exercised in an organization. As a result, other techniques of motivation, discussed in the previous chapter, are needed to supplement the efficient delegation of authority in order to realize desired objectives. For example, a subordinate may be delegated the right to call employee meetings for purposes of generating employee participation in his section, in addition to other rights which may be delegated to him to achieve a particular set of objectives or tasks. *Whatever the delegation of authority, it must be clearly specified to facilitate the achievement of the duties assigned.*

3. *Accountability.* This depends on two factors. The first is the attitude of the person to whom duties are delegated. The second is the dependability arising from such an attitude. Let us review an actual example of delegation to clarify the impact of these two factors.

> Stanley S. was assigned the duty of finally checking and reviewing all bids sent to customers by the management of a foundry. It was his responsibility to check the bids for misstatements, mathematical errors and omissions, and to maintain a master file. One day, Bill J, the sales manager, noticed an order that appeared to be grossly underpriced. On pursuing his investigation, Bill found that the bid submitted to the customer had a mathematical error amounting to several thousand dollars. Confronted with this situation, Stanley explained that he sometimes gets the bids in batches, and is always under pressure from the sales representatives to get the bids out. Occasionally, when he still has a batch of work on hand at the end of the week, he gives it a quick look and sends it out. Otherwise, he would have a big backlog and problems from the sales representatives for losing orders because of late bids.

In the above situation, while assigning the duty of checking bids, the crucial aspect of accountability was overlooked. The attitude and dependability of the employee were both unfavorable. This could have been taken care of by the management by either assigning this task to a more conscientious and dependable individual, if available, or by putting the attitude and accountability of the employee in question in the correct perspective. This could have been done by clearly specifying what his priorities in checking bids should be, and that he would be held accountable for any errors that pass through his scrutiny of the bids. Clear accountability certainly helps in guiding the individual to have the right perspective in which he must perform.

Therefore, in the process of delegating tasks, the manager must co-relate and clearly specify the duties, authority and accountability involved to the different members of his group. Contrary to the popular management belief that authority and responsibility must be equal, it is seldom possible to delegate authority to its ideal extent. Under such conditions, it is clear that employees receiving obligation are accountable to fulfill their duties to the maximum extent one can reasonably expect, in light of their authority and work situation. You must also keep in mind that accountability may be reassigned and redistributed, but cannot be delegated. In other words, as a manager you may assign tasks in your group, delegate the corresponding authorities necessary and specify accountability, but you are still accountable for the achievement of the tasks and the group's overall performance. It is beneficial, therefore, to have a system whereby you get continuous feedback about what is going on. The feedback may take the form of daily or weekly reports, periodic verbal reports, work sampling checks and on the spot visits. This will enable you to know of delegation problems in advance so that you can overcome them.

HOW TO SET YOUR SPAN OF CONTROL

How many subordinates reporting directly to a manager can be properly supervised? This problem has been discussed a great deal by management practitioners and authors. Colonel Urwick has recommended that a single manager in the higher levels of management can effectively manage six individuals directly subordinate to him. In addition, he may have a number of other employees reporting to him for purposes of coordination.[3] Others have recommended a span of between five and ten. Yet a number of

---

[3] L.F. Urwick, "The Manager's Span of Control," *Harvard Business Review*, Vol. 34, No. 3, pp. 39-47.

eminent managers feel that the span of control concept is no longer valid. Under this diversity of views, what guidelines can and should you follow?

Experience has shown that the problem is not capable of a general solution, since so much depends on the variety of functions involved and the nature of the organizational setup. For example, in the Sears Roebuck Company of America, a vice president may have a hundred stores under him, each being an autonomous unit responsible for marketing and for profits. Each store manager, in turn, may have thirty or so section supervisors under him, running their own individual autonomous units and being responsible for marketing and profitability goals. This larger span of control is possible because of the high degree of decentralization and delegation. Each unit handles much of their work under delegated authority, so that the important matters which need to be taken up are sufficiently few in number, and therefore can receive personal and immediate attention. Such spans of control have worked very successfully for Sears Roebuck.

There are three main reasons for the success of deliberately planned large spans of control when accompanied by decentralization and delegation:

1. In such situations, there is a lower number of hierarchical levels and a short chain of command. This generates greater organizational efficiency, since each hierarchical level tends to distort objectives, misdirect attention, cause delays and serve as a source of inertia and friction.

2. Decentralization and delegation leads to each unit performing and contributing directly to the overall objectives of the group or organization. This makes performance measurement easier and more motivating.

3. This arrangement gives great scope for the increase of the individual initiative of employees. It gives people actual responsibility in an autonomous position when they can gain and develop from such an experience. This tends to develop employees for subsequent positions of greater responsibility. This is dramatically illustrated by the following actual experiment by a large American corporation.

A large number of young men were hired by a big retail business organization. About one third of them were put in each of the following three areas—large stores, small stores and mail order business. The large and small stores were autonomous units responsible for marketing and profitability. The mail order business was organized by functional specialization. Five years later, a study of how the different groups of employees had progressed in the organization showed startling results. The more capable amongst the young men in the small stores were becoming managers of the small stores themselves. In the large stores, the best amongst the young men were getting to be section managers. In the mail order business, there had been expansion and new openings. However, the best men had left the company and the others were still clerks.

Span of control based on decentralized responsibility and authority helps to develop the best employees, and at the same time provides an efficient framework for the achievement of group and organizational objectives.

What guidelines should you follow in setting your span of control? Broadly speaking, two main guidelines emerge from the above discussion.

1. *Make the chain of command as short as possible.* This means reducing or limiting the hierarchical levels as far as practical. In order to do this in an effective manner, the second guideline becomes necessary.

2. *Put the promising and deserving employees in autonomous positions* by decentralizing duties and authority and assigning corresponding accountability. The greater the decentralization, the shorter the chain of command. Through the process of delegation, you can enlarge your span of control, and still provide the required personal attention and time required for important issues and supervision.

Depending upon the capability of the available personnel, the more a manager follows the above guidelines, the more efficient his span of control will be.

HOW TO RELATE THE UNITY OF COMMAND TO YOUR OBJECTIVES

Henry Fayol, the well known proponent of management principles, was the first to emphasize that an employee should receive orders from one superior only. [4] Such is the rule of unity of command. When this is violated, authority is diffused, disciplines

---

[4] His original work, "Administration Industrielle et Generalle," first appeared in 1916. Its translation is "General and Industrial Management," Sir Isaac Pitman & Sons Limited, London, 1949.

undermined and stability jeopardized. Modern experience has shown that it is not always possible or advantageous to follow this rule indiscriminately. Let us, therefore, see what course you should follow in relating the unity of command to your objectives.

First of all, let us see what causes the existence of dual command in an organization or group. It is a common occurrence, and can cause havoc in all organizations or groups, large or small. It exists in the garb of apparently justifiable pretexts. There are three such common situations in which dual command tends to plague any organization.

1. A superior may give orders directly to an employee without going via the employee's direct supervisor. Thus, a production manager may give orders to a machine shop employee without going via the machine shop supervisor in charge. This may be done to gain time, to put a stop to an undesirable practice, to relate better to junior employees, etc. If this practice is repeated often, dual command will exist. This may generate a number of ill effects, such as hesitation amongst subordinates, dissatisfaction and irritation in the supervisors or managers bypassed, disorder and disruption in work schedules, etc. Does this mean that as a manager you should never directly order employees in your group without going through their direct supervisor? No, not necessarily. It is, however, important that when such a situation does become necessary, the supervisor or manager concerned must be informed in writing or verbally, as the situation warrants, to make him aware of the latest situation. Mutual consultation with the individual supervisor or manager concerned is desirable prior to taking action, but where that is not possible it should be done as soon as practical.

2. The dividing up of authority between members of a family, colleagues, friends, etc. is often avoided on the basis of mutual regard, common interest and confidence that good sense will always prevail amongst them. This results at times in dual or multi-command in an organization or a group.

Over time, however, awkwardness and irritation are felt, and sometimes dual or multi-command generates hatred against the sources of authority. People cannot bear dual or multi-command and its resulting vagueness, particularly over long periods of time.

An early assignment of duties, authority and accountability in an organization or group contributes greatly to the achieving of set objectives by them.

3. The natural intermeshing and overlapping of functions in an organization or a group can lead to dual or multi-command situations. This happens particularly when duties are badly defined, leaving room for duplication of effort and command. As a manager, you can assist your work group to achieve organizational objectives successfully by assigning duties and authority clearly to follow natural work flows, taking particular care to separate and differentiate areas of responsibility and authority in overlapping functions and duties.

In all human associations, such as in industry, society, home, government, etc., dual or multi-command is a source of conflict and deterioration. Notable exceptions are research oriented groups and organizations. There, the unity of command loses much of its importance due to the nature of the organizational environment necessary to promote research objectives. In general, however, the unity of command principle should be followed as a guideline as far as practical. It must be practiced with considerable flexibility to suit different organizational entities and situations. In many organizations, it may need to be bypassed on a short term basis for purposes of emergencies and organizational urgencies. Nevertheless, communication to those individuals bypassed must be made to maintain coordination and morale.

The unity of command principle guides the clear assignment of duties, authority and accountability, and thereby aids the efficient achievement of organizational and group objectives.

THE IMPORTANCE OF MAKING SURE YOUR OBJECTIVES ARE UNDERSTOOD

After you've initiated the management process and established objectives, organized resources, delegated tasks, made spans of control more efficient, and related the unity of command to the achievement of set objectives, there remains an important activity which you need to carry out in order to ensure the successful achievement of desired objectives.

You must check that organizational and group objectives are clearly understood by all employees. This is certainly an obvious and fundamental activity, yet in actual practice it is most often neglected or overlooked. When this happens, individuals work toward different interpretations of set objectives, which leads to conflicts of interest and an inefficient and diverse effect of individual efforts. As a manager, therefore, you will certainly stand to gain by making sure that your organizational objectives are clearly understood by all members of your work group.

What is the way to do this with the least amount of time and effort? The following three steps will assist any manager to accomplish this both effectively and efficiently.

Step 1. Convert all objectives into tangible goals and subgoals on a time scale, i.e., both short term and long term. Use the process of employee participation [5] wherever possible to accomplish this step.

Step 2. Communicate and discuss these goals and subgoals with all those responsible for accomplishing the goals or subgoals. Individual subgoals must be endorsed either in writing or verbally by the individuals concerned. It is very important to set individual subgoals under mutual consultation and ask for endorsements of subgoals thus arrived at. It is at this time that hidden objections and difficulties are voiced by employees. Most of these objections and difficulties stem from misunderstandings and lack of information, and can easily be clarified by the manager. When there is a real difficulty, it is beneficial for you to be aware of it, so that you can either replan or overcome the difficulty through the resources of the organization. When endorsements are not asked for, employees tend to avoid speaking out, and hence the manager is not made aware of real and misunderstood difficulties till it is too late. Furthermore, endorsements by employees tend to motivate them to achieve what they have agreed to, which serves to improve the overall performance of the work group. Endorsements of subgoals may be asked for in the form of weekly or monthly plans, in the form of a memo, or verbally, depending upon the nature of the organizational activity and the importance of the subgoals. What is most important is that all concerned individuals be asked to endorse the subgoals for which they are made responsible. While establishing and getting subgoals endorsed, it is important to discuss these subgoals in relation to the total group and organizational objectives. This will enable employees to keep the overall group and organizational goals in mind, thereby choosing the best alternatives and activities to accomplish their own subgoals within the organizational context.

Step 3. Review and inform individuals as to how they are performing in relation to plans. In every dynamic organization, goals

---

[5] This has been discussed in Chapter 2 in the section 'understanding employee motivation.'

and subgoals constantly need to be updated and reviewed. This review of past performance should be discussed in detail with all individuals responsible for achieving subgoals. In these review sessions, employees would get an opportunity to clarify their doubts and air their difficulties. Often, misunderstandings would be clarified and subgoals put in the proper perspective. It has been found that feedback on the past and current performance of individuals tends to motivate 'them to improve and correct their efforts, which helps them meet objectives and further clarifies them in their minds.

By following these three steps, you will not only make sure that your organizational objectives are understood, but you will also help to motivate employees to accomplish their own individual tasks efficiently, thereby leading to the achievement of desired work group objectives.

Chapter 4

HOW TO MAKE YOUR EMPLOYEES MORE CREATIVE

Why is it necessary to make employees creative? Creativity, in an organization in today's competitive world, is not something which can be ordered or bought. It is advantageous to encourage innovation and original ideas from your people on the job, as well as to hire consultants for specific creative projects. Your work group knows the needs for betterment and the needs of the organization in a manner no one else does. Their creative ideas have a much higher success rate than the ideas of outsiders. Many professional conferences have dealt with this subject because the need for creativity in all organizational activity is steadily increasing.[1] Basically, employee creativity may be explained "as the ability and potential to produce original works or ideas on the job." Thus, an employee can be described as being creative if he initiates or suggests action *which has never occurred before*. He is uncreative if his actions break no new ground.

In today's competitive environment the emphasis is shifting from manual work to creative work. This means that, more and more, an employee is expected to create output by using his knowledge, experience and brain rather than merely the brawn of his muscles.

It has been recognized that an organization's capacity for innovation and its ability to foster and sustain creativity is a key

---

[1] A well known three day conference, held at Harvard, on "Creativity in an Organizational Setting," attended by 70 of the world's best known creative minds from business, education and government, dealt with this question in detail.

factor contributing to its success and strength. While creativity can not be ordered in employees, fortunately it can be stimulated, motivated and induced. We shall see in this chapter how this may be done. Researchers have established that creativity is not exclusive but can be developed in degree by all people. Creativity is God-given and the wonderful thing is that everyone has it to some degree. Few of us, however, have trained and exercised it to anywhere near its full potential.

EVERYONE CAN BE MADE MORE CREATIVE

Creativity exists in all individuals, but in widely varying degrees. The main deficiency exists in that people do not utilize their creative faculties. In the organizational context, what is important is not the extent to which employees have creativity, but the extent to which their creative potential is utilized. This is illustrated in the following example.

The manager of a sales department, Joe B., was surprised to learn about the interest which one of his dullest clerks, Ed C., had in fine printing. Ed had his own small press at home, on which he turned out good work. Joe B. had the clerk transferred to the company's small printing operation, where he developed several cost saving schemes and improved the quality of the printing output considerably. Once Ed was given the opportunity to utilize his creative talents, he was no longer a dull employee. Ed showed a great amount of creativity—but in printing—not sales.

Recognizing the fact that the capability for creativity exists in all of us,[2] let us see how the existing creative potential in employees can best be utilized.

IMPROVING THE CLIMATE FOR CREATIVITY AMONG YOUR PEOPLE

The psychological setting in an organization has a direct impact on the functional creativity of its employees. As a manager, before

---

[2] Kenneth A. Kesselring, a successful innovator and manager of General Electric's Knolls Atomic Power Laboratory, has conveyed that the harnessing of atomic power would not have been made so practical but for the creative input of many employees at all organizational levels.

you can get into the techniques of making your people more creative, you must ascertain whether the climate in your group is favorable towards encouraging individuals, psychologically, to make productive contributions in their daily tasks.

As a manager, you can improve the climate for creativity through the following three steps:

1. *Assist in overcoming individual insecurity.*

Personal feelings of insecurity tend to block an employee's creativity on the job. These also tend to reduce general productivity and effectiveness. As a manager, you can be instrumental in reducing, if not eliminating, personal feelings of insecurity by helping such employees to develop self-confidence. This can usually be done quite effectively by giving employees individual assignments of responsibility to suit their potential. An application of this is illustrated by the following example:

> Ralph S., the administrative manager of a large organization, put Mrs. Charlette Y., an efficient young woman, in charge of a stenographic pool. He had been aware of her innovative and creative potential when she had served as his secretary. However, Charlette lacked confidence in being able to coordinate and manage the stenographers in the pool, and expressed her anxieties. Ralph S. emphasized his confidence in her and quieted her protests. He was aware that she had never been given an independent assignment and that previously, in the home and office, she had been dependent on someone else for final decisions. However, since Charlette had exhibited that she could come up with creative solutions in panic situations, he reasoned that all she needed was to develop her own confidence. He abruptly put her on her own in handling the stenographers' pool, delegating to her the responsibility and authority to administer the pool, and telling her that whatever decisions she took would stand. It took a few days for her to overcome her doubts, after which she settled down as an efficient supervisor, managing the workload imaginatively and handling the girls efficiently to everyone's satisfaction.

Managers who encourage insecure employees to speak their minds without fear of criticism, ridicule, or fear of losing face help to bring out more and more creative actions and solutions from them.

> Hugh J., the sales representative of Household Appliances, was nearly fired for lack of satisfactory performance. Luckily for him,

before this could happen, his boss was replaced by a new sales manager, Tom G. Tom encouraged Hugh to try out new ways to increase sales. In fact, Hugh had been thinking of promoting a program to sell several different household appliances as a package, rather than concentrating on one product at a time. He had never mentioned this innovative idea to his old boss for fear of criticism. But Tom was encouraging and understanding. He supported the packaged household appliance program, which was a great success in that it boosted sales of Household Appliances by 42%. Hugh's creative selling idea could be utilized only when an appropriate climate for exchange of ideas was generated by his sales manager.

The overcoming of individual feelings of insecurity not only spurs creative output among employees, but makes them do their day to day work with greater effectiveness as well.

2. *Removing work oriented blocks to creativity.*

In practically every organization, there is some tendency to resist the unfamiliar. Even new ideas are resisted if they are really non-conformist. Conformity to practice is both a social and organizational malady which blocks creative tendencies. Even when we think that we are being progressive and open to new ideas, we tend to squash good ideas for a variety of work related reasons. Some managers don't want to disturb the status quo. Others view some ideas as a threat to their own position. Some managers erroneously believe that their own ideas and solutions are the best of all, and still others don't want to stand out and attract attention.

As a manager then, what should you do to encourage creativity on the job and still not conflict with work and organizational objectives? The answer lies in analyzing whether you tend to squash ideas for any reason other than lack of merit. If you do, then you can profit by analyzing and suppressing your personal prejudices. Generating, recognizing, supporting and implementing innovative ideas in the work environment is a distinctive attribute of every successful manager. These creative and innovative ideas will emerge in your group if you don't let work related blocks, such as conformity, resistance to change,[3] lack of flexibility, and pressure for short term results prevail in the job environment. This is illustrated in the following example:

---

[3] See Chapter 10, which analyzes why employees resist change, and how their resistance can be overcome.

All shoe manufacturing machinery used to be painted black in the U.S.A., till a few decades ago. The reason? It had always been that way. A supervisor of a shoe manufacturing plant noticed that one of his experienced operators was having trouble with his eyesight, and therefore, with his production. The black machinery and the black leather offered hardly any contrast. The supervisor instructed the machine to be painted a light grey. But the operator was not happy, as he felt that a different colored machine would look odd. A lighter color than black would show the dirt quickly and would need to be cleaned more frequently. The machinery should be black, since that was traditional, he protested. Nevertheless, the supervisor said that they would try this out as an experiment, and requested the operator's cooperation. He agreed, but felt ill at ease till the operator at the next machine asked for grey, too. In the meantime, the first operator increased his output noticeably, and realized that his eyesight wasn't bothering him any more while working on the machine. Another operator in the plant suggested painting all moving parts red for purposes of safety. This idea was implemented and picked up by other manufacturers. Today, machinery is available in a variety of colors for operational ease and aesthetic considerations.

To create the right climate for creativity on the job, a manager should not reject ideas and solutions generated in the work group that seem ambiguous or don't appear to be directly related to the problem at hand. It is from such ideas that brilliant solutions are often found. This makes the time spent in keeping ideas flowing well worth the effort.

3. *Overcoming environmental blocks to creativity.*

We have reviewed how the manager can improve the feelings in individual employees and improve the job routine to encourage creative thought and action. Another critical dimension to be improved is the physical environment and the scope of organizational activity.

If physical facilities need to be improved to get the optimum productive and creative output from a group of employees, then the manager should inititate and propose such action without delay. Otherwise, the manager is likely to be blamed for not having brought this to the attention of his superiors earlier. When presented positively, with emphasis on benefits likely to accrue from improvement in physical facilities, the proposal is likely to be well received. Such a move is also likely to boost the morale of the employees concerned and result in improved performance. A manager's superiors may not realize that a bad condition exists, or that existing circumstances bother employees, unless a proposal is properly presented.

Creative managers change the environment to remove limitations imposed upon them. This may be a physical move (like improving facilities), or may be a change in the scope of activities.

> Coca Cola originated as a patent medicine. It was realized by creative managers that it had limited sales potential. Their marketing activity overcome this limitation by promoting the pleasant taste of the beverage to make it world famous as a refreshing soft drink. This creative idea led to others in promoting the sales of the beverage. To introduce this new taste, they gave away free Coca Cola in schools and other public places. This was very effective in creating a huge demand for the drink within a short period of time.

As a manager, you can use the preceding three steps to set the climate for creativity in your work group. To further enhance this climate, the process of sensitivity training can be used to improve working relationships and understanding within the work group.

USING SENSITIVITY TRAINING TO IMPROVE RELATIONSHIPS

Getting a group of employees to work together smoothly and effectively is sometimes more complex and difficult than other managerial functions, such as planning and control. Interpersonal problems which arise on the job can not be ignored. These problems are frequently due to factors and causes which people do not acutely understand, and they need to be tackled if an organization is to function at a high level of effectiveness.

One way to handle the job of improving teamwork and effectiveness in the group is to institute a sensitivity program for that group within the organizational framework.

A large number of problems on the job result from misunderstandings, attributing one's faults to others, and from lack of a free flow of communication between different persons within the group.

These problems can be overcome through sensitivity training by resolving tension and conflict between individuals, and making them more sensitive and understanding to each other in the work situation.

The objective in this kind of training program is primarily toward awareness of self, of others, and of interpersonal relations, rather than toward the acquisition of management theory or principles. When such awareness at both the emotional and intellectual level occurs in a work group, it brings about a favorable change in work attitudes and behavior. Experience has indicated that working together on initial problems of interpersonal relations results in a stronger and more cohesive work team.

The sensitivity training program

The sensitivity training program of a working group has the following features:

1. *Relative lack of a planned agenda:* The actual content of the training sessions is highly flexible. External time pressures to discuss things according to a rigid sequence are nonexistent. The participants are asked to deal with problems which are rarely, if ever, introduced in conventional work oriented meetings. Discussion is focused on the clarification of interpersonal perception and relationships within the group, rather than on technical job issues.

2. *Frequency of meetings:* Two hour sessions, once a week for about six weeks, is generally adequate. The number of sessions is flexible, and meetings should be held till a breakthrough in interpersonal communication and understanding is experienced.

3. *Leadership of meetings:* Work group meetings are generally chaired by the high status person in the group. However, in the training sessions the object is to have "leaderless" or free discussion as far as possible. The trainer, who is generally an outside person experienced in sensitivity training,[4] has a minimal role to play in discussions. He is more of a coordinator, and guides the discussions toward the objective of the training sessions. Other than that, he has no words of wisdom to preach. Nevertheless, considerable planning is necessary on his part in setting up and carrying through the training program.

---

[4] Such trainers are either management consultants or certain qualified faculty members of a College of Business Administration. In rare cases, the manager himself may be the trainer, if he has sufficient experience in sensitivity training.

4. *Attitude preparation:* In the vertical structured training group, each individual would naturally tend to protect his status, security and power. However, for sensitivity training sessions to progress and be successful, the group manager must be willing to accept criticism, otherwise, little interchange of opinion is possible. The outside trainer may need to hold private interviews with the group manager to allay his fears. Other private interviews by the trainer or group manager with individuals who are threatened by the training process might also be necessary before the training program can progress. Once the correct attitude and perspective regarding the training sessions is generated, they can be highly successful and satisfying in generating self-perception as well as inter-personal understanding amongst the group members.

The description of sensitivity training and how it works can best be conveyed through a narrative to illustrate the steps involved in a successful sensitivity training program.

Hank W., general manager of the Goddard Sewing Machines Company, had a tough problem. He had just accepted, from the president of the company, the responsibility of introducing an advanced automatic sewing machine model in the market within four months. He knew he would really have to get his plant working in clockwork fashion to get this accomplished. The key people would be William M., head of design and engineering, and Ted P., head of production, and their assistants. Unfortunately, Hank had noticed a rift between Bill and Ted. They always seemed to have differing points of view, and apparently didn't get along as well as Hank would have liked. He couldn't afford any foul-ups in this project. He wondered whether they should still go ahead with the "sensitivity training" sessions, which Art N., the management consultant, had suggested would help create a more cohesive work team, by getting everyone working together in a group on mutual problems of interpersonal relations. Since he realized that the plant was always going to be under pressure, he decided to go ahead with the two hour per week sessions. This might be the very thing to make the current project a successful one.

The first meeting was stiff and even a little tense. Art had explained that the meetings would be informal and there would be no specific objective, except to explore problems of common interest. A few suggestions came up about what to discuss, such as office memos, line of authority of the plant to the home office, and why everything needed to be referred to the home office, etc. However, there was very little discussion as such. When the meeting was over, there was a general feeling of apathy and vagueness.

At the second meeting, the group became concerned about getting the sessions productive. Hank and Ted dominated the discussions which followed the earlier suggestions. It was clear that the group was not ready to work at the real problems.

The third and fourth meetings were exercises in frustration, since the discussions of the theoretical topics were proving impossible. Ted pointed out that he thought the meetings were getting nowhere. Art suggested that everyone look at the reasons why this was happening. He urged everyone to speak their mind on some of the real day to day interpersonal problems they faced.

The fifth meeting brought a change in the pattern. A few cautious remarks, by Steve L. and Grady J. of the production department, were made about how it was difficult to freely discuss production problems with Bill. The talk was a little more open, and nearly everyone seemed to want to talk at the same time. The fifth meeting ran fifteen minutes over the usual two hours.

In the sixth meeting, Bill asked for concrete examples of where others had found it difficult to communicate with him. Steve and Grady explained that they had occasionally felt themselves cut short by Bill when discussing a design related production problem. They explained that this did not mean that they didn't get the right answers to most problems from Bill, but that it left them with solutions to parts of the problem and not the whole system. Bill said that he wasn't aware that this was what they felt, as his attempt would always be to tackle the whole issue rather than in parts.

Jim and Rick, assistants to Bill, brought up the problems they faced in getting noncommittal answers on design improvements from the production department. Hank was impressed to see Rick speak up and put the problem in a sensible, logical way. He had always thought that Rick was too quiet and self-contained. Was it possible that he had underestimated Rick and his capabilities? Art noticed that the barriers were falling. People in the group were learning to listen and talk to each other about their fears of, and feelings for, each other. They were becoming sensitive to their own needs and to those of others. They were beginning to accept each other, not for what they would have liked each other to be, but with all their strengths and shortcomings, as they were. As the meeting drew to a close, Art noticed that the atmosphere was more relaxed than it had ever been before. He knew that the barriers had been broken, and now the management of Goddard Sewing Machine Company was on its way to becoming a team. He knew that now in regular staff meetings, the members of the group would not avoid discussing and clarifying real problems in an open manner. With time, the awareness and understanding initiated in the training sessions would be continued to generate greater cooperation and teamwork in the group.

Communications in the work group can be improved vastly as a result of the sensitivity training sessions.

Sensitivity training thus is a tremendous tool to improve working relationships on the job and to increase the free communication of ideas and problems between the members of a work group.

Let us now see how the creative process can be initiated in your work group under a favorable climate for creativity and free communications.

THE CREATIVE PROCESS IN YOUR GROUP

Most people can be creative without knowing exactly how they do it. However, many truly creative people approach the process of creativity quite systematically. An understanding of the technique used by effective and successful creative individuals can certainly assist managers in initiating the creative process in their work groups.

The creative process in the work environment consists essentially of five basic steps.

1. Orientation of the problem or objective facing the group.
2. Obtaining the facts.
3. Searching for ideas.
4. Letting the ideas incubate.
5. Evaluating the ideas.

Let's look at what each step involves.

ORIENTATION OF THE PROBLEM OR OBJECTIVE

This is the most crucial step of the creative process. Orientation of the problem or objective implies that you look deeper into the problem or objective rather than accept it at its face value. Many managers have great capabilities in terms of job knowledge, experience, etc., but are mediocre performers because they accept problems and objectives on their face value, and tackle them doggedly but without much success. An example will make this clear.

A large manufacturing organization became concerned about rising absenteeism among its skilled workers, of which there was a general shortage. The administrative manager, Art T., looked at the problem as one which obviously required tightening control over the employees. The perils of absenteeism were made clear in the house organ, and stern lectures were given at work group meetings, urging employees to be more responsible. There was little improvement in the situation, and the basic problem of high absenteeism continued. During this time, there was a transfer among the managers, and a new administrative manager, Bill S., was assigned to the manufacturing plant. Bill studied the problem of absenteeism. He met with the group of skilled workers where absenteeism was the highest to determine the cause of their high absenteeism. There were several reasons, but the prevailing one was that this group of employees was most sensitive to health considerations, and felt that management was insensitive to their needs. Periods of illness and disability were prolonged because of delays in getting proper medical attention, making timely claims, and in general because of taking a day or two off to recuperate periodicially from the continuous strain of work. Each employee knew how far absenteeism would be tolerated, and they went as far as it would. The scarcity of skilled workers made them aware that their jobs were pretty secure. Having understood the basic causes of absenteeism, Bill decided to bypass the usual unsuccessful approaches to the problem and tackle its various aspects. He initiated a system whereby all employee absences were recorded and reported daily. Arrangements were made on a selective basis to visit the hospital or employee's home to determine the degree of an employee's disability, and in general express the company's interest in the employee's welfare and early recovery. Assistance was also provided in the preparation of disability claims whenever employees were eligible. This reduced absenteeism, and instilled in the employees the belief that the company was genuinely aware of their health needs and welfare.

The manager in the above example could produce results in solving the problem by analyzing it in some detail. He discovered that part of the problem was that employees thought the company didn't care about their health needs. By implementing a solution to account for the real causes of the problem, excellent results were achieved.

To obtain better orientation regarding your problems and objectives, it is necessary to analyze them with group participation wherever practical. It helps to list every factor you can think of that could be a part of the problem, and look for the key factor. Then it is necessary to divide the problem into the smallest parts possible, and concentrate on elements of the problem you yourself can control. Many managers orient the problem or objective naturally, and may not be even aware that they follow the above steps. Analyze your own approach and see if it conforms to the above. It is quite likely that to a great extent it does. If not, then you can benefit greatly in improving your creativity and effectiveness by orienting the problem or objectives to the existing situations as discussed above.

OBTAINING THE FACTS

The group must next tackle the task of getting *all* the relevant facts possible. The challenge lies in knowing when you have enough. There are three indicators to determine this:

1. When you have numerous repetitions in your further search for facts.
2. When new data comes in very slowly.
3. When you run out of time or money to gather more facts.

The facts must be verified for validity. This can be done easily by observation to confirm reported or researched information, instead of accepting its validity without question.

A group involved in the development of new products discovered from the plumbing codes of many cities that it was forbidden to install garbage disposal units in the kitchen sinks of homes and apartments. The group thereupon concluded that a good market existed for portable garbage disposal units that did not have to be installed in the plumbing. The product was introduced and failed. This was because the company had not verified the facts by actual observation. An inexpensive random sampling of the homes in targeted cities would have shown that many home owners were ignoring the codes and installing conventional units anyway, because the cities were rapidly changing the codes to permit the plumbing installation of the conventional unit.

The above example illustrates the need to verify all the facts gathered by the work group, however certain and conclusive they may appear at the outset.

SEARCHING FOR IDEAS

In searching for ideas, you can start with the problem or objective, select a key attribute, and consider different approaches toward introducing it. Generally, the key attribute or advantage is borrowed from the outside, sometimes from what may appear to be an unrelated situation.

> For years, the manual typewriter served a useful purpose. Then product development groups looked to key attributes which could be added on to the conventional typewriter to meet the needs of faster and better quality reproduction. This resulted in the typewriter being electrified to make it easier to use and to give it greater flexibility with increased number of type sizes and styles. Next, the typewriter was developed so as to serve as a typesetting device. The ideas of programming were incorporated to introduce the MTST,[5] which can automatically type letters at very rapid speeds from preprogrammed cards, in addition to serving as an ordinary electric typewriter. Thus, several attributes from other sources were added to the typewriter to make it something more versatile and useful.

This search for ideas can essentially be divided into three steps.

1. *Knowing specifically what you seek.* One can not get far with general objectives. The specific objective or objectives must be pinpointed. Thus, making the typewriter more capable is too much of a generality, but making the typewriter type automatically from programmed input, or to add typesetting capabilities to the typewriter, are action oriented objectives which lead to creative results.

2. *Select the key attribute.* The next step is to select the key attribute. This follows directly from knowing specifically what you seek. In the case of the typewriter development, a key attribute would be inexpensive programmed typing.

---

[5] Magnetic tape set typewriter introduced by IBM.

3. *Analyze different approaches to realizing the key attribute.*
The different approaches to introducing the key attribute now serve
to crystallize the creative search for ideas: Paper tape, punched
cards, magnetic tape, etc. are the different approaches which
required analysis in the advent of programmed typing.

An important aspect in searching for ideas is to use analogies or
parallels to serve as the source of ideas. The idea of programming
the typewriter emerged from the programming applications of the
computer. During the idea gathering group sessions, behavioral
scientists have found that employees should be encouraged to
bring up anything that comes to mind about the problem in hand—
analogies, parallel situations, science fiction ideas, role playing in
terms of equipment parts, etc. which could bring up ideas from the
subconscious mind. The use of the subconscious mind in such
sessions is encouraged, since it is capable of uninhibited creativity.
These ideas need not make sense to start with. They are initially
recorded, and then sifted by a committee to select a few ideas worth
following up. These are then discussed in the work group in order
to arrive at a tentative course of action. The advantages of this
approach are many. Often, fresh insights are provided by apparently unrelated analogies to arrive at creative approaches.
Through the process of group participation, a great variety of
aspects are looked into, resulting in a well balanced and overall
view to creative action. Furthermore, the participation of individuals in searching for ideas motivates them towards the implementation of the final suggested solutions or objectives.

LETTING THE IDEAS INCUBATE

After having searched for ideas and arrived at a tentative course
of action, it is advantageous to let the ideas mature and fill out. A
few weeks incubation time before taking a fresh look at the selected
ideas, in order to enlarge them and polish them for implementation, is well worthwhile.

As a creative writer puts it—let us think of enlarging our true
and fresh ideas, and as soon as we get an idea or half idea, let's not
find ourselves running out with it into the street, trying to make it
rule there. Our ideas will in the end prove more useful after
maturing a little. This was illustrated in the example of the portable
garbage disposal unit. The idea was not permitted to mature or

expand, which precluded the possibility of determining the real need of garbage disposal units. Instead of rushing into the manufacture of portable garbage disposal units, had the policy of allowing a week or two for maturing all ideas been followed, there would have been time to analyze the present and future potential for garbage disposal units.

At the end of the few days of the incubation stage, the ideas should be evaluated to see if they still look good. Those ideas which do should then be evaluated in comparison to each other and in terms of implementation requirements.

EVALUATING THE IDEAS

The ideas should then be ranked according to general criteria, and possible improvements and constructive suggestions should be considered before arriving at the final course of action.

The suggested course of action should then be evaluated in terms of what will be required to implement it. Is it feasible? If so, is the trouble going to be worth it? Some brilliant ideas may fail this test. Ideas must be feasible in terms of the organizational resources to make them valuable. The next question is whether the course of action is feasible in terms of the timing considerations. If the idea looks attractive after evaluation, in terms of the above considerations, then you are ready to put it into operation with a reasonable certainty of success.

SELLING YOUR IDEAS TO ACHIEVE CREATIVE ACTION

Ideas not acted upon are useless. It's using them that counts. In other words, you have to sell ideas constantly to people at all levels of the organization. This requires creativity. In fact, the selling of ideas that lead to creative action often is more difficult than originating the ideas.

Contrary to what some people may think, in general, good ideas *do not* sell themselves. Most of the world's well known inventors struggled all their lives to sell their ideas. The Wright brothers could not interest the U.S. Government in supporting experiments for a flying machine. Galileo's ideas about the nature of the universe led to his persecution for heresy. Chester Carlson could not find any support for his invention of Xerography[6] for numerous years. He was turned down by about a dozen organizations, all of whom then entered the market at a disadvantage after Xerox Corporation made Xerography one of the most profitable inventions of all time.

It is, therefore, important to not only generate good ideas but to be able to sell them as well.

A lot of work and research has been done on the different ways of putting ideas across successfully. Based on this past experience and research, let us now see how best to actually sell ideas. After an idea is considered workable, the following approach has been found to be the most effective.[7]

Step 1. State at the outset the most significant benefits of your idea. People are interested in facts and features of an idea in terms of what *benefits* it can provide. Stress these benefits, and then correlate facts and features to show how these benefits will accrue. These benefits must be in response to real needs. Discuss benefits and needs and use facts and features to show how. Facts by themselves are not enough.

Step 2. Probe for specific interests and needs which can be met by your idea. Don't assume that you know all about the needs of the situation and the real interest of the people to whom you are selling the idea. Get them to talk about what they are working for, what their interests are, what they view as priority needs, etc. Listen! Some of these interests and needs you would have anticipated. But let the person or persons you are selling the idea express them. Once the needs have been expressed, show how your idea can meet some of these important needs. This way your idea will have greater impact after showing how each need can be fulfilled. Ask for and get agreement from those concerned.

Step 3. Answer objections. Anticipate possible objections. Rehearse answers to these in advance of the confrontation. This will help you to be well prepared for answering actual objections when they arise. Many ideas have been sold at the initial stages because their originators anticipated objections and reactions and how they would suitably respond to them. Always rephrase the objection as

---

6 Literally translates from the Greek to mean "dry copying." This is the process used by Xerox Corp. in all of its masterless copying and duplicating equipment.

7 This approach has been tested by actual selling results, and is used in the imparting of professional selling skills.

you understand it before you answer it. This has saved unnecessary misunderstandings and misinterpretations of a voiced objection. The objector may mean something quite different to what the listener (you) may think he means. The surest way to avoid this discrepancy is for you to rephrase the objection by using an expression such as the following—"If I understand you correctly, your objection is that...."

Very often, if the objection is a weak one, the rephrasing will serve to show to the objector that it is really not an important consideration. If it is a real objection, then by rephrasing and getting the objector's "yes," you can attempt to answer it and overcome it with factual explanations wherever possible. If this cannot be done and it is a genuine obstacle, then you will have to modify your idea or proposal to accommodate it in order to get it implemented. Rephrasing an objection before answering it is therefore important for the following reasons:

1. It confirms what the actual objection is to both parties. In case of a misunderstanding it clarifies the real objection.

2. It prompts the objector to qualify an incomplete or unclear objection, and to provide additional information where required.

3. It helps to answer weak objections.

4. It generates a feeling of better understanding and genuineness about your concern for the needs of the situation.

The whole idea can be misunderstood if you do not rephrase objections to clarify them, but tackle them as perceived by you.

It is just as important to reinforce positive acceptances and agreements to the benefits provided by your idea. At the time of reinforcing an agreement, it is advantageous to further expand the agreed-to benefits. One way to do this is as follows: "Yes, this will certainly provide a more efficient performance from our sales force. In terms of actual benefits it will mean higher sales and lower inventory, which means we would be operating with reduced storage costs." The first sentence reinforces agreement and the second expands the benefits of the idea.

Step 4. Summarize benefits. After answering objections, take the initiative to review and summarize the benefits to be provided by the idea. Authorization for implementing the idea may be asked for after the benefits have been summarized in a number of ways, depending upon the situation. It may be asked for directly or indirectly. The indirect approach assumes authorizations and asks questions pertaining to the implementation of the idea. For example: "Is it better to implement his idea this month or next month? Where do you want this idea to be implemented first—in the assembly plant or the foundry, etc.?" When you ask for or assume acceptance of your idea, two things can happen:

1. You will get agreement or,
2. You will not get agreement.

In both instances it is important to follow through.

Step 5. Follow through: If acceptance of the idea is gotten, it is important to follow up to see that the idea is, in fact, implemented. If, on the other hand, agreement is not forthcoming, it is necessary to find out the real objection or objections and start again from Step 3. Each objection should be restated and answered. Alternately, the idea should be modified to accommodate valid objection. After this, the benefits should be summarized and acceptance of the idea asked for directly or indirectly, as best suited to the situation.

Getting through to people and getting ideas accepted is, to say the least, not easy. To make headway, one can benefit from remaining cool and following the cyclical five steps outlined above. Take your time to follow these steps fully and you will succeed in getting your ideas accepted.

ORGANIZING THE CREATIVE PROCESS

Can managers organize the creative process? Yes, they certainly can. In fact, all successful managers knowingly or unknowingly organize their group so that they can tap the creative resources available to them. You can organize the creative process in the following manner by:

1. Organizing for creativity
2. Generating creative ideas
3. Managing creativity

1. *Organizing for creativity:* There are four approaches which can greatly improve the organizational climate for creativity; (1) *Broaden spans of control:* There is really no ideal number of people or sections of people a manager should supervise. Nevertheless, in the past, organizations have tended to keep the number small, resulting in a longer pyramidal structure with many levels. This has inhibited creativity because of the distortion, diffusion, delay and frustration in the transmittal of information through long chains of command. By broadening, and thereby flattening, the organizational structure, people at the top and the bottom come closer together. Communication lines shorten, participation

emerges and creativity improves. See if you can shorten lines of communication in your part of the organization. (2) *De-emphasize status:* This will greatly speed communications and creativity. To do this, encourage contributions of suggestions and exchange of ideas from all organizational levels, recognize the contribution of individuals at all levels, use voluntary contributions both from inside and outside the work group for special assignments and projects with no hierarchical bias, and make management, in general, and yourself, in particular, more visible and accessible to all individuals in your work group. (3) *Delegate and decentralize:* As one who is interested in creative output, you can certainly benefit by practicing delegation and decentralization. Give individuals freedom from organization restraints to apply their talents to needed solutions. Encourage project teams and exchange of decentralized responsibilities whenever practical. (4) *Tailor the organization:* There is nothing sacred about existing organizational structures. As needs and environment are constantly changing, you should change your organizational group to fit changing circumstances. It is futile to fit people into stereotyped jobs. It is much better for organizational productivity to modify the organization to fit the people. This, in general, serves to tone up the organization, and assists in tapping the creative resources of different individuals.

Having adapted the organizational structure to aid creative output, let us review how you can generate creative ideas.

2. *Generating creative ideas.* If a project or problem requires various disciplines, it is beneficial to generate creative ideas collectively. There are various techniques which can be used in collective creativity.

The two man team: A two man team works best in a problem involving two disciplines, or when a combination of judgment and imagination are necessary in a fairly straightforward manner.

Brainstorming: This is a popular technique used in the generation of ideas. It dramatically makes participants experience the impact of collective creativity. The guides to having a brainstorming session are:

- The group should be comprised of about 8 to 10 people.
- Encourage expression of many ideas without evaluation, i.e., ideas expressed need not seem logical or practical to start with.

- The ideas brought forth should not be evaluated in the session.
- Combine and improve ideas. Let others build on the ideas already expressed.
  Keep the session working as one group—do not let subgroups form.
- Maintain a friendly atmosphere in the session.
- Make problems as specific as possible. Multiple problems should be avoided.
- Strive for quantity in ideas, as well as quality. The more ideas you have the better the chances of a brilliant solution.

Evaluation of ideas should come after the session. Brainstorming is a good technique to get you moving. It helps to assure you that you are overlooking nothing about the solution of a specific problem. An individual or a smaller group needs to be assigned to follow up on the brainstorming session. The advantages of brainstorming to generate ideas are demonstrated by the following example:

A controlled experiment was conducted by Carborundum Company, in which one group worked jointly on ideas to use idle equipment, while another group attacked the problem individually. The group working together and using the brainstorming approach turned up 44% more worthwhile ideas than the other group using solo ideas.

You can use the "brainstorming" approach to generate creative ideas in your work group for tackling difficult problems with no obvious solutions, as and when the problems arise.

The X-committee. This is a special group assembled to work on a specific problem or a series of closely related problems. When the solution is implemented, the group disbands. Fairly complex problems go to such ad hoc groups. The X-committee can also be formed to follow up ideas generated by brainstorming or other means.

Tim L., the general manager of a large sewing machine factory, was worried about the decreasing profitability and increasing costs of its manufacturing operations. Prices of sewing machines could not be raised because of the stiff competition existing in the domestic and world markets for sewing machines. Costs of raw materials and components were rising at approximately 10% every year. This had changed the one time highly profitable operation of the sewing machine factory to a loss situation. The factory faced a critical challenge in meeting the situation. In order to tackle the problem collectively, a cost reduction committee was organized. This committee was composed of all the department heads and a few other enterprising and promising employees. Dick S., a relatively young executive who showed great promise, was assigned to coordinate and implement the cost reduction ideas generated from this committee. A number of material substitutions, design changes, production efficiencies, inventory reductions, purchase efficiencies and labor savings were suggested and introduced which would not have been possible through individual efforts of each department. Creativity and communication were spurred through the cost reduction committee. A 15% savings in operating costs resulted, which contributed directly in increasing the factory's profitability. The committee's formation was instrumental in salvaging the situation through collective creativity. This set the basis for the factory to diversify its products, and improve its operations progressively in the future.

Synectics: This is a technique for getting ideas promoted by Synectics, Inc. At the heart of the technique are insights into the psychological nature of creativity. The unconscious mind has clues to problem solutions which must be retrieved and formulated by the conscious. A synectics session is a controlled attempt to do the retrieving. Problem solvers are encouraged to oscillate between a rational consideration of the specific problem and a search for nonrational analogies. It permits people of diverse disciplines to communicate in common everyday language.

A typical session begins by acquainting the participants with aspects of the "problem as given," or PAG. The group converts this into the "problem as understood" (PAU), which is a tentative approach to the problem selected for discussion. Then the group coordinator asks the group for a "direct analogy" (DA), which should be an object or phenomenon brought to mind by the PAU. Too exact or obvious analogies should be avoided. The group may be asked for personal analogies (PA), i.e., get the members to pretend they are an object in the problem and to express how they feel in such a situation. The personal analogies are combined to form a symbolic analogy (SA). This helps to release the participants from viewing the problem merely in terms of previously analyzed elements. This series of analogies forms what synectics calls an "excursion." If one approach fails to bring up a desirable solution or worthwhile idea, the technique allows for more "excursions." The group finds other analogies, or takes one of the unused ones and starts the DA's, PA's and SA's once again.

What the above technique has demonstrated is that in generating collective creativity, you can use analogies to great advantage. Comparing the problem under discussion with similarities to solutions in the everyday life and world, howsoever unrelated, can be very helpful. The following example illustrates the usefulness which a simple analogy can provide.

> Clay S. had been plagued by the problems generated by the filing system used by his predecessor. It was difficult, if not impossible, to find anything he wanted from the department files. He called a department meeting to discuss how the filing problem could be improved to meet the needs of all concerned. He opened the discussion to ideas, and encouraged his employees to express their experiences where they had noticed efficient filing systems. Mary J. pointed out that her cooking club had a very efficient way of keeping track of recipes. She suggested filing by categories, with alphabetic order within each category. Like the cooking club—they didn't file apple pie under A, but under P for pies. It was a simple and efficient system. Thus, the department got a new filing system which worked well, thanks to the analogy expressed by one of its employees.

Combination of techniques: A number of other approaches, such as "think tanks," programmed invention," etc., are modifications or combinations of the above techniques. You may adapt or combine these yourself to achieve collective creativity in your work group.

3. *Managing creativity:* How does a manager go about managing creativity? First, he needs to forecast the innovations needed both on a short-term and long-term basis. Ideally, these should be a part of his work group's overall objectives. The need for new and better solutions to problems provides tremendous scope for creative objectives. Developing employees also lends itself to creative approaches in matching training inputs with individual needs and potential.

As a professional manager, you have to constantly direct the forces of creativity into the most productive channels. By planning, organizing and implementing creative action in your work group as discussed here, you will not only make your employees more creative, but also motivate and manage them to successfully achieve organizational objectives.

AVOIDING THE DANGERS OF CREATIVITY

Creativity is not without inherent dangers. You can avoid the dangers by noting the following.

1. *Test your conclusions.* Avoid haste in accepting what appears to be a wonderful idea. Be skeptical about what seems a perfect solution till you test it out fully.

A well known tire company introduced, with great publicity, a new kind of tire. It aimed to corner the market with the sudden innovation introduced. After the tire was introduced, it was discovered that it fell apart when driven at high speeds at regular intervals. The hasty "creative" action cost the firm heavily in terms of replacement costs and prestige.

2. *Avoid ego involvement.* Guard against rationalizing away the unfavorable aspects or results of your idea. Discourage ego involvement of any individual in your work group with his or her creative idea. Look at each idea solely on its merits, and not as to who presents it. Creative ideas are not monopolized by highly intelligent people. Employees who are mediocre and not excessively sharp may present creative ideas or solutions in a situation where more intelligent colleagues are still guessing. Watch out for the self-styled creative expert, particularly one who has a record of some success with creative ideas. An example will illustrate.

Steward Y., a young executive in the sales department of an automobile company, had successfully suggested a number of cost saving ideas. He then came up with an idea that involved reorganizing the complaint handling service. His superiors had some mild objections, but Steward sold his idea on the strength of his past successes. The reorganization was implemented. The idea was based on developing specialists to deal with different categories of complaints, thus reducing the staff. The staff was reduced, but the complaints about getting satisfactory service increased tremendously. The specialists were juggling customer complaints among them in "a pass the buck" routine. More people had to be assigned to fill in the gaps, resulting in an overall increase in the complaint handling staff as compared with before the reorganization. Steward's involvement with his own ego had blinded him to the failings in his idea. The company learned the hard way that each suggestion should be looked at on its merits alone.

3. *Don't maintain fixed ideas about creativity.* There are popular theories which relate creativity with irrationality and wildness. Some believe that true creativity can spring only from undisciplined and free wheeling individuals. Still others believe that men are more creative than women, Caucasians more so than Negroes, younger people more so than the old, and so on. These theories have holes in them and no scientific merit. Even more logical theories, such as the one that creativity requires a high intelligence level, have been disproved. Research has shown that creativity can be high even in a person with a mediocre or low IQ. Creativity can turn up in the most unlikely people and situations. Thus, danger exists if you maintain fixed ideas about creativity. By keeping an open mind, you can provide the right creative climate for your work group and avoid pitfalls based on superficiality.

4. *Relate creativity to need.* Not all creative ideas are useful. This is a danger which goes unnoticed till it is too late.

A gas company, in its drive for innovations and creative ideas, nearly went out of business when it realized that its new 16 slice conveyorized gas toaster, conveyorized gas oven, food warmers, etc. did not appeal to restaurant owners. What appeared as brilliant innovations failed in the market place. A market survey and test at the initial stages would have saved the company from pursuing a costly and fruitless course of developing products without sufficient demand.

Before any creative ideas are implemented by your work group, research its need and benefits. Good ideas should not be pursued merely because they are good, but because they will meet and serve a real need. It is therefore wise to devise ways to test the usefulness of ideas in advance.

Pioneer Tool and Oil Company built a baitless, odorless, automatic mousetrap that could catch mice by the dozens. It was compact and automatically led the mice to a waterfilled compartment where they drowned. Pioneer built 5,600 of these wonderful traps out of which only 400 were bought by customers. The traps were good but expensive, and failed to sell. [8]

Creativity can be dangerous—unless the ideas it produces are modified and *adapted to serve* estimated real needs.

---

[8] This was reported in the *Wall Street Journal* of March 6, 1967.

Chapter 5

HOW TO INSTRUCT
AND INFORM YOUR PEOPLE

A manager's effectiveness depends to a great extent on his ability to communicate with different people at all levels of the organization. As a manager, therefore, you can benefit from improving your ability to communicate with people. The following paragraphs contain suggestions and examples on how this can be done.

SAYING WHAT YOU MEAN, EVERY TIME

Some people find it hard to express in words what they mean to convey. Others can put across their message only after repeating information already conveyed and using a lot of extra sentences. The reason is not merely that some people are more gifted than others in their ability to express themselves. By and large the more important factor is that some people are better "thought" organizers than others. They think out what they have to say before saying anything important—particularly where prior preparation is possible—such as before meetings, interviews, negotiations, speeches, etc. It is certainly possible for everyone to learn and make a habit of organizing one's thoughts before saying them. This helps in improving communications and enables you to say what you want to. It is a good rule to say what you mean instead of beating about the bush or throwing hints. Frankness and straightforwardness pay in dealing with people, particularly when they are coupled with politeness.

The following four steps are necessary to say what you mean every time. These steps are valid for all types of communications, such as instructions, speeches, discussions, circulars, etc.

Step 1. Think out in advance the main objectives or key points of the communication you want to make.

Step 2. List down all related points you want to cover.

Step 3. Anticipate questions and objections and think of answers to clarify them.

Step 4. Make sure that all that you wanted to convey has been covered in your communication with the intended audience. This is easily done with the help of the earlier Step 2. These four steps form the key to effective communications by all successful managers. Some practice it consciously and deliberately, whereas the more gifted ones do it with ease as a matter of course, without any extra effort. As a manager, do you take these four steps consciously or unconsciously before making any important communication to any intended audience? Chances are that you do to some extent, but not every time. By making a commitment to yourself that you will cover these four steps in all important communications, you will be able to say what you mean, *every time.* This will not only improve your efficiency and effectiveness, but that of your work group as well.

UNDERSTANDING YOUR AUDIENCE

It helps to communicate in terms of the motivational interest of others.[1] Most people overlook this obvious need. They generally tend to communicate in terms of their own needs or on the basis of facts alone. Unfortunately, such an approach does not get as much results as one in which the listeners' motivation to accept is involved. An example will serve to illustrate this:

Alex T., the marketing manager of an air conditioning firm, had unintentionally antagonized the manufacturing manager, Mark M. This had happened in an instance where a prospective customer had wanted certain modifications made on one of the standard products.

---

[1] Douglas MacGregor, in *The Human Side of Enterprise,* was one of the first to point out the obvious need to consider what motivated individuals in a work situation. For a review of the five levels of motivation, please see Chapter 2.

Mark had resisted this. The matter had gone up to Bob J., the managing director for arbitration, who had ruled in favor of marketing. This had generated a bitterness between the two departments. Now Alex was faced with a touchy situation. The Hilliard Construction Company was interested in ordering air conditioning units for an apartment building they were constructing, if certain modifications were made in the standard units. The order in itself was not large, but would lay the foundation for much larger future orders. This would be the first order from Hilliard Construction Company, and Alex didn't want to pass up the opportunity to get a foot in the door. At the same time, he didn't want to heat up the existing bitter relationships, but rather wanted to cool them down. He reviewed the situation and decided to present it in a manner which would incorporate the motivational interest of the manufacturing manager. He appealed to the self-esteem of Mark in the following manner while explaining the situation to him:

"I've got a request for another one of those special jobs again. I've had no luck in trying to argue Hilliard Construction out of these modifications. I wouldn't even consider this order if it wasn't for the fact that Hilliard Construction is going to do the big high rise job next to the park, which could mean an order 4 times this size. The project engineer, whose name is Watanabe, insists on these modifications. I've explained to him the problems these changes create for us. I couldn't convince him, as I couldn't really discuss all the technical modifications which he was suggesting. I therefore asked him to come and see someone who really knows what his suggested modifications would entail—you. When you see him, maybe you could explain our position better and make him see the light."

This approach fitted Mark's higher level need for self-esteem. He agreed to the meeting and suggested that the engineering manager, Steve A., also be present. As things turned out, they persuaded Watanabe to drop a few of the more troublesome modifications, and agreed to incorporate the less difficult changes. Alex had learned enough about his audience in the factory to communicate in a manner which incorporated their interest and motivational needs.

Therefore, in understanding your audience, you have to ascertain how things are viewed by them and at which motivational level their need is the greatest. Communications should then be made incorporating the viewpoint and motivational interest of the audience.

CONSIDERING YOUR OBJECTIVES AS YOU SPEAK

Planning is useful only if implemented. Similarly, objectives are achievable if not lost sight of. A few of us get so wrapped up in conversation and the way it drifts that we forget to bring it in line with our objective till it is too late. A simple everyday example will illustrate this point.

> Stan J., the administrative manager of a large fan factory, had become a close social friend of Bill S., the general manager. A day before Bill was to go on vacation, Stan walked into his office to dispose of a few matters before he went on leave. Stan wanted a few sanctions which affected his department. To lay the framework and appeal to the motivational interest of Bill, he initiated a personal friendly discussion. The conversation got involved in the working of a club of which they were both directors. Time flew, and soon it was time for Bill to leave. Stan then hastily presented his proposals. He got a friendly reply to most of them. "Al, I think these can wait. Let's discuss these when I return." Stan couldn't say no to his friend and boss, even though he would have liked his proposals decided upon before Bill left.

The above example is typical of many everyday occurrences which delay the achievement of set objectives, however major or minor they may be. The effective individual knows that in his communications, he has to have his priorities clear—his objectives come first. Motivational interests must be incorporated to achieve the objectives. They cannot in themselves become the ends. The administrative manager, while speaking to his general manager, relegated the objectives of his visit to other considerations to his own disadvantage.

KEEPING YOUR EMPHASIS POSITIVE

While communicating with people, compliment and praise them whenever you can do so honestly. The negative should be ignored or touched upon carefully when it becomes necessary to do so. When this happens, the criticism must be made in as constructive a way as possible. It should not be dramatized or exaggerated, despite the very natural human tendency to do so. If at all it should be done realistically and honestly, in as polite a manner as possible.

Syd S., the marketing manager, had been having trouble with Tom G., one of his section heads in charge of customer complaints and claims. Tom was highly qualified. He had a law degree which he had earned while working with the company by going to night classes. Consequently, he thought he knew more about his work than his boss, and so would argue on various issues. It became a problem to get anything done through him, as he had all sorts of legal and procedural points to throw at Syd before moving on with any assignment. During a company reorganization, Syd took the first opportunity to have Tom transferred as a part of the newly formed sales liaison department. The sales liaison manager, Bill T., sized up the strengths of the newly transferred section head and gave him greater autonomy than he had ever experienced before. He conveyed to Tom that it was an asset for the new department to have such a well qualified person. To recognize his capability, he was given the opportunity to meet deadlines and demonstrate his worth. With this positive approach, the once troublesome section head became a cooperative and efficient member of the work force, contributing to the success of the new department and its manager. Thus, Bill had emphasized and utilized the strengths and positive aspects of the problem employee, and had minimized his negative habits to motivate him into becoming a productive member of the department work force.

Every individual has both positive and negative attributes. By emphasizing the positive attribute of individuals in organizational communications, you as a manager can motivate others to cooperate and perform effectively.

DOING WHAT YOU TELL OTHERS TO DO

It is essential to follow up on communications and do what is expected of you. Your reputation for fairness and honesty is difficult to acquire, but easy to lose—and this is one of your most valuable assets in dealing with and managing people.

The most common tests of credibility are in the little things. Do you expect others to meet deadlines, when sometimes for various reasons you don't? Do you pass the buck? Such actions, however cleverly done, fool almost no one for long. It is important, therefore, to establish your credibility in order that people respond to you without reserve and suspicion. Obviously, if you want others to meet deadlines and not pass the buck, you must demonstrate that you work by these rules yourself. This will motivate others to emulate you when you interact with them. Employees are known to shift their behavior and pattern of working to suit the nature of their boss. If they are working under a manager who follows the rules he sets for others, they consider it fair to follow them, too. However, the same people will not follow the same rules willingly and sincerely when they find that their boss himself is not personally committed to them. This is so obvious, yet in actual practice, so often overlooked. Managers often expect individuals in their work force to do what they say—meet commitments, deadlines, assignments, etc. Occasionally, however, due to time pressures, they themselves promise to do something and then find that they cannot. This is certainly not appreciated by others, and should be avoided. Make only those commitments which you are reasonably certain of acting upon. If you cannot do something which you promised to do, inform the concerned individuals and explain why. Say what you can do under the changed circumstances. Always follow up promptly on your commitments by either doing what you said you would, or saying what you can do if circumstances have changed, or if you do not intend to act on some request, say so and explain why.

TELLING A ROUNDED STORY

While communicating with people, failure to give all the pertinent facts or to distort them can lead to problems. It is essential that you convey all the necessary facts in order to get the proper response from people. This is not only true for complex and important subjects, but also for common day to day matters as well. For example, while ordering or instructing a person to do something, tell him why. When you make a request, give the significant background on it. It has been found in motivational studies that people tend to do things better when they understand the full story behind what they are doing.

Ed F., the manager of an automobile manufacturing plant, had been concerned with the productivity of his machine shop workers. Productivity fell further when the design of some components was altered. Ed decided to discuss the situation fully with the workers concerned. He called a meeting and explained the reason for the change in the component parts. He pointed out that these changes would make the automobiles safer and reduce exhaust pollution. He further emphasized the contribution which the machine shop workers would thereby be making in helping to turn out better automobiles. The expected increase in corporate profits would also mean more money for them via the existing profit sharing plan. But this could be achieved only if they kept their competitive edge in the market place by keeping the costs of production down through efficient productivity levels. Lastly, he explained that the changed components their machine shop made were the key to the improved design of the car, which was the first of its kind to drastically reduce air pollution through car exhausts and thereby meet an urgent social need. By telling a complete or rounded story, Ed produced an appreciable increase of 27% in the productivity in the machine shop. This was because the workers now had pride in knowing the role they were playing in producing an important innovation.

You can easily determine the favorable impact of telling an individual or individuals the reason behind a rush job or an important assignment. Next time you give instructions for something to be done, take a few moments to explain the background on it where ordinarily you wouldn't have done so. Then see how much more willingly and happily your instructions are carried out.

PUTTING YOUR POINT ACROSS WITHOUT WORDS

Eyes, gestures and facial expressions sometimes say more than words can. In all cases, they can complement and reinforce the message which one is trying to convey.

Research in business communications has indicated that non-verbal communications, such as those conveyed via the gesture, posture, face and eyes have an important bearing on how the message is interpreted by others. The same words spoken with fidgety hand gestures will have a different impact than when spoken reassuringly with confidence. Sometimes the difference in impact can be crucial. More and more, business organizations are training their personnel, particularly in the sales areas, to communicate effectively in terms of both verbal and non-verbal communications in the area of face to face communications. This is done by recording role play situations on video tape, which is then replayed. Individuals are often surprised to see how they appear to others in meetings, negotiations, interviews, selling situations, etc.

Mannerisms such as frowning when one becomes disturbed over something, sitting in a slumping manner, showing anxiety by leaning forward, twitching or pursing of the lips, etc. are observed to exist by people who were completely unaware that they had such mannerisms. Once observed, such mannerisms can usually be corrected easily.

To use the above training technique for your personal benefit, practice role plays which you are generally faced with in front of a mirror. You will be clearly able to identify any undesirable mannerisms that you are presently unaware of. You can then easily avoid them and practice improvements in your facial expression, eye movement, posture and gestures to improve your overall personal impact in face to face meetings with people.

Listening is an important part in understanding the situation and putting your point across accordingly. In face-to-face meetings with people, the more effective managers spend more time listening than talking. What is your proportion? If your self-analysis reveals that you talk more than you listen (which is perfectly natural), then you can make yourself communicate with others better than you do now. In order that you get to listen more in your conversations with people, ask questions, invite opinions, show interest and restrain boredom or impatience. Don't interrupt. Let others finish what they have to say before you handle an objection. You may cut them short and never deal with the real or complete objection. People with high levels of intelligence have to be particularly careful in making an effort to listen. Otherwise their intelligence usually prompts them to summarize a situation and communicate their intelligent analysis without trying to really go into the situation. This can prove to be a costly error, as they may miss the crux of the problem or situation altogether.

> The head office of the ABC Manufacturing Company had experienced problems in getting correct accounting data from one of its factories. Pete J., an accounting expert, was sent down to the factory to correct the situation. He really knew the ins and outs of financial and cost accounting, and demonstrated this in discussions with the factory's accounting personnel. He pointed out what, in his opinion, needed to be done to improve the works accounting system. He redesigned new cost accounting records and financial statements and, after being thoroughly satisfied, returned to the head office. Despite his expectations, there was no appreciable improvement in

the correctness or timeliness of the accounting statement. Cost data as reported did not conform to actual costs, even though he had set up a fairly comprehensive and elaborate cost accounting system. The managing director was upset and sent another one of his account managers, Tom S., who was relatively new in the organization, to the factory to set things straight once and for all. Tom did not go in as a "know it all" who had come to show the work's accountants how things should be done. Instead, he asked for what problems they were facing, and said that he had come to help them out wherever he could by eliminating or reducing their difficulties. He listened to complaints, difficulties and suggestions on how to improve things. He discovered that the loophole lay in the present system of inventory pricing, which did not reflect the actual cost of production. Having pinpointed the real problem, he incorporated the suggestions of the work accountants to update the inventory pricing records, and introduced a new procedure which would reflect the actual costs of the materials issued to production. Once this was done, both the correctness and timeliness of the accounting reports from the factory became a matter of routine. Perhaps Tom did not know as much about financial and cost accounting reports and forms as Pete did, but he certainly knew how he could be more effective in a new situation—by listening as much as possible.

The purpose of listening should be entirely selfish. It should be to understand the situation completely or uncover what the others say which would assist you in handling the situation to the advantage of all.

ENCOURAGING FEEDBACK INFORMATION

You will not succeed in communicating well with everyone all the time. There is nothing to worry about as long as you learn from such experiences and seek feedback on how you can communicate better under these situations.

Keep your office door open at least part of the time so that others will come to you. Let people know you are interested in their ideas and thinking. Follow up, observe and seek feedback on the effectiveness of your communications. This is particularly helpful when you are having difficulty in communicating with any individual, when misunderstandings have been created, or when you simply want to clear the air. The following is an example where a manager did this to great advantage.

John S., the sales manager of the office products division of XYZ Corporation, felt a communication gap arising between him and the engineering products sales manager, Henry L., despite his attempts to communicate and set up inter-divisional procedures between the two divisions. He could feel a bit of resentment and tension in the air whenever they met. Both product groups had to complement each other as they often had common customers. Therefore, their mutual cooperation was necessary, particularly in customer relations and for promoting new business from prospective and existing common customers. Was the greater success and better performance of the office products division a source of antagonism to Henry? A little unlikely, John thought. He decided that he had to clear the air, and so arranged for a meeting with Henry. When they were alone together, John expressed what he had been feeling and invited Henry to express himself frankly about how they could improve the situation. Henry opened up and pointed out where he felt he had been "one-upped" by John, particularly in handling some large accounts, where office product equipment was placed first, restricting and delaying the sale of engineering products. This was based on a simple misunderstanding, which John clarified by showing the instructions he had received from the marketing director to negotiate with the customers in question first for office products. Due to an oversight, Henry had not been informed of this. They both then arrived at a mutual working arrangement and enacted a practical system whereby they would feed each other with business prospects on a continuing basis. They also settled on a system to deal with new customers. This not only helped to clear the air, but increased the cooperation between the two selling divisions.

By encouraging feedback of information, you not only help to clear misunderstanding, like the office products sales manager did, but also pave the way for increased future effectiveness. This becomes an important input in instructing or informing people successfully at different levels of the organization.

Chapter 6

HOW TO GET THE BEST RESULTS FROM YOUR PEOPLE

In managing people, successful executives have found the following to be true:

1. *It pays to gear efforts to results rather than to work.* This means focusing on the contribution which each of their team members (superiors, colleagues and subordinates) make and can make to achieve desired goals. They start by establishing individual contributions rather than the work to be done and its techniques and tools.

2. *Best results are obtained by building on strengths—their own strengths, the strengths of their superiors, colleagues, subordinates and the situation itself.* They do not let weaknesses or things which cannot be done distract their efforts.

3. *To get superior performance and outstanding results, they concentrate on a few major areas.* They set up priorities and follow through on their priority decisions. They know how to make meetings effective as well as productive by using the principle of contribution. They clarify the purposes of meetings before holding them, and see that these are achieved.

4. *To execute effective decisions, they know how to balance democratic behavior with getting "tough" when necessary.* They tailor-make their team leadership to suit different situations.

The above four approaches can enable you to get the best results from your people. Let us now see how these approaches can be put into operation in any organizational setting.

FOCUSING ON THE CONTRIBUTION OF EACH MEMBER

The focus on contribution is the key to getting the best results from your people. You have to ask yourself how best you can contribute in your present position to the organization. How can your subordinates, colleagues and superiors contribute individually in their relationship with you and yours to them? What can be the contributions from meetings, reports, and the management tools and techniques you apply? The organizational mechanics, chain of command, office procedures and all efforts in themselves are of no avail. It is the results from efforts which matter. Hence with every individual in your team, with every situation, with every meeting and, in general, with every organizational activity it is necessary to think about contributions rather than efforts.

Despite the obviousness in the logic that results should be emphasized over efforts, most executives get wrapped up in matters of authority and their own efforts. This is illustrated in the following case example.

A well known management consultant rates executives quite accurately from the answers he receives to the following question: "What do you do to justify your being on the payroll?" The great majority answer in the following manner: "I am in charge of the sales force," or "I have 900 people working under me," or "I run the administration department of the company." Such answers stress downward authority and focus on efforts. They do not reflect results or contributions. Those executives who are on their way up and have a history of success look upon their jobs differently. They are likely to say the following: "I am responsible for meeting the targeted sales of the company's products and generating customer satisfaction," or "I am responsible for the efficient production of the company's products," or "It's my job to give our managers the information required to make the right decisions!" During the course of his interviews, when he finds executives focusing on contribution and responsibility for results, he recommends them as "top management" material. Accordingly, the persons who focus on efforts and stress their downward authority are "subordinate" material, no matter how high their title and rank, as they do not hold themselves accountable for the performance of the whole.

The focus on contribution turns the executive's attention away from his own specialty and his own department, and toward the performance of the whole. Such an executive is likely to think about what relationships his skills, function, specialty, and department have to the overall organization and its purpose. As a result, what he does and gets others to do will not be out of phase with the organization's main objectives.

In dealing with your immediate group of subordinates, as well as with various other individuals in the organization, good working relationships are important. Focus on contribution in your own work. This will make relationships productive—which is the only way to have good working relationships. Pleasant words and warm feelings are meaningless, if there is no achievement, in a work focused and task focused relationship. On the contrary, an occasional rough word will not damage a relationship that is based on results and accomplishments. In a study of successful managers who inspired deep devotion and true affection in all who worked for them, Peter Drucker points out a common trait—all of them built their relationships with their superiors, colleagues, and subordinates around contribution.[1] Not one of them worried about "human relations." Their emphasis on productive working relationships took care of that. In fact, this common emphasis by otherwise widely differing managerial personalities made them well renowned in industry for their wonderful ability to manage people and keep organizational morale high.

To establish contributions from subordinates, it is best to take a direct approach. You can ask your people for answers to the following questions: "What are the results for which you feel you should be held accountable? What should be expected of you? Can your knowledge and ability be utilized better?"

These questions can be asked in the form of a questionnaire to all employees, and the answers can be discussed with each employee in individual sessions. You, of course, will have the right and the responsibility to judge the validity of the proposed contribution. You may be amazed to find that the objectives set forth by some employees will project opportunities and results far in excess of what you would have set. Such increased targets, whenever feasible, should be supported. You will also benefit in this exercise from being made aware of how your employees view needs and opportunities. This common sharing of mutual concerns will bring you and your group in better contact, and make your job of

---

[1] Peter F. Drucker, *The Effective Executive*, Heineman: London, 1967, pp. 53-54.

establishing individual contribution goals more effective and realistic. Ask the same questions of yourself. Such an action will foster individual self-development both of yourself and of others. By focusing on contribution, employees will in effect be questioning themselves as to what self-development they need, what additional knowledge and skills need to be acquired, what personal goals should be set, etc. Others will thus be stimulated to develop themselves, whether they be subordinates, colleagues or superiors. It has been found that people grow according to the demands they make on themselves. Focusing on contribution serves to do this in a practical manner for both yourself and all others you work with.

When you inform your superiors and colleagues as to the contributions you have undertaken to make, it will require them to gear themselves up too, if that is necessary. Teamwork in your own work group will also increase, as people will now be concerned with others using their output for it to become effective.

Thus, by focusing on the contribution of each member in your work group, including yourself, you have a tool to get the best results from your people.

BUILDING ON EVERYONE'S STRENGTHS

To get optimum results from people, a manager must use all the available strengths—those of his subordinates, associates, superiors and his own. To make these strengths productive is the key to individual and organizational success. Every individual is abundantly endowed with weaknesses. The manager's efforts can make these largely irrelevant by using the strength of each employee as a basis for joint performance. The most practical way of using employee strengths is in the process of staffing.

Staffing for Results. Staffing decisions are crucial decisions. All results are obtained through the most important organizational resource—high calibre people. The better this resource is allocated to contribution areas or opportunities, the greater the achievement of desired results. For the maximization of this resource, it is necessary to practice the following principle:

"The top calibre employees must always be allocated to major opportunities or tasks."

A manager must not try to exploit major opportunities with anything but top calibre people. If this resource does not exist, the manager must get it or develop it from within existing human resources. Similarly, top calibre employees should never be assigned to anything but major opportunities. If none appear to be available, the manager must seek or develop new ones.

All this is easier said than done. It is not easy to staff for performance because of human likes and dislikes, personal considerations, the temptation to diffuse top rate resources rather than to concentrate them, etc.

Staffing for performance therefore requires you to impose on yourself the discipline of an objective staffing method called the "forced-choice" method. To use this approach, you need to take the following steps:

Step 1. Draw up a list of major opportunities (tasks) and assign a ranking to each in terms of contribution to desired results. Each opportunity must be ranked without ambiguity.

Step 2. Rank your people resources by their ability to perform. All top calibre, mediocre and marginal employees must be ranked consecutively.

Step 3. To the highest ranking opportunity or task, allocate all the high ranking human resources that it requires. The next ranking opportunity comes next, and so on. Low ranking opportunities are not to be staffed at the expense of a higher ranking one.

The ranking of people and opportunities or tasks becomes the basic decision in this method of staffing for results.

Once the people and opportunities are matched, efforts can be taken to structure the work organization so as to make strengths productive and weaknesses irrelevant. Let us see how some managers have implemented this approach.

Walter S., an accounts manager, hired a good tax accountant who was known to have been greatly hampered in his private practice by his inability to get along with people. Walter saw to it that the tax expert got an office area of his own, and initially designed the work flow so as to shield him from direct contact with other people. The organization saved a record amount in taxes the following year, because the strength of a key employee was concentrated on a desired result opportunity, and his weakness was made largely irrelevant by the "staffing for results" approach of an effective accounts manager.

Building on the strengths of individuals and work teams has thus been a success pattern followed by effective managers in generating optimum performance through their people.

THE IMPORTANCE OF CONCENTRATION

There are so many different areas of importance that the day-by-day method of management is no longer adequate. It has become necessary for every manager to reduce the almost limitless possible tasks to a manageable number. Because of so many demands, there is need to *concentrate* important resources on the greatest opportunities and results. In other words, it has become necessary to do the few important things right and with excellence. This can be achieved only through concentration of both people resources and time to produce optimum results.

We have already seen that you can benefit from concentrating your top human resources on major opportunities or tasks. In the area of time resources, you can get best results by concentrating on doing one important thing at a time. That is the only way the majority of people can achieve excellence in the accomplishment of major opportunities. Concentration of effort is necessary precisely because there are so many tasks clamoring to be done. By doing one thing at a time, the result is doing it fast. The more you can concentrate time, effort and resources, the greater the number and diversity of tasks you can actually accomplish. Let us see how one successful executive used the principle of concentration to get optimum results.

Arthur B., a management consultant retained to advise on organizational structure revision, was particularly impressed with the way Peter Y., the general manager of the organization, managed his time. The sessions Arthur had with Peter were neither too short nor too long, being about 1 1/2 hours each. This was a big enough chunk of time to cover everything important, and short enough to avoid repetitious discussions. During these sessions, there was never a telephone call or any personal interruption. Peter's secretary had been told to hold anything but immediate crises situations which couldn't wait 1 1/2 hours. So far there had been none. Arthur also discovered that the general manager had a very effective way of consolidating and concentrating chunks of time for major issues and productive tasks. All meetings, reviews, problem sessions and so on were scheduled for two days a week, on Mondays and Thursdays. The mornings of all other days were set aside for consistent work on major issues and productive tasks. The afternoons of these days were left unscheduled for whatever might come up. Of course, many things did come up, such are urgent personnel problems, visits by important customers, a trip, an emergency production meeting, etc. It was in the mornings of three days a week that Peter concentrated his time on major result producing issues alone, which made him a highly effective manager.

The manner in which managers concentrate their discretionary time on productive issues is not important—it is the fact that they do that matters. Effective managers control their time management continuously. Let us review the steps involved in doing this.

Time Management & Concentration: The process of time management and concentration involves the following four steps:

1. *Know where your time goes.* Before you can attempt to manage and concentrate your time on productive issues, you must know where it goes. The best way to do this is to record how your time is spent. You can do this by keeping a time log yourself, or asking your secretary or assistant to maintain it for you. A two week analysis of your time log will show you how little of your time is being spent on productive matters, and how great a time is being taken up on unimportant and unproductive tasks.

2. *Prune time wasters.* Dispense with tasks which have no bearing on results, where nothing of significance would happen if you didn't do them. There may be speeches, committee memberships, meetings, etc., that contribute little or nothing to your own organizational activity which may be dispensed with. If there are any in your existing time schedule, don't hesitate to say "no" to them. If you value your time, others will, too.

3. *Delegate tasks.* Estimate what tasks could be done by someone else just as well, if not better, and transfer such tasks from your own work schedule to those who should really be doing them.

4. *Consolidate and concentrate time on productive tasks.* Set aside time in appreciable amounts to be concentrated on major issues in order to produce optimum results. Small increments of time on major issues will lead to inefficiency and mediocrity, if not worse. Time must be concentrated in large, continuous and uninterrupted units to accomplish productive and significant tasks.

Thus, the process of concentration in both the areas of people resources and time provides for optimum results.

SETTING PRIORITIES

It is important to concentrate and do one thing at a time, but one must know which things to do first and in what priority.

Generally speaking, work pressure determines which things are done first. When this happens, important tasks get sacrificed. Pressures always concentrate on yesterday or the past. Results exist in the future—past achievements and problems should no longer preoccupy the effective manager.

The best way of setting priorities is to do it the hard way, i.e., by first deciding what tasks not to tackle. This is not easy. It is much easier to draw up a nice list of top priorities and then hedge by trying to do a little of everything. This is likely to make everyone happy. Nevertheless, nothing gets done. In order to concentrate efforts, human resources and time on result producing tasks, the lower ranking or irrelevant tasks must first be eliminated. A task which appears to have no significant impact on the future should be eliminated without fear, as only one of the three things can happen:

1. Nothing.
2. It is attended to in time automatically during the course of another result producing task.
3. It becomes an important issue in the future, and is attended to.

Of course, it is necessary to be objective in eliminating tasks—future impact, and not unpleasantness of the tasks, should be the decision criteria.

Having eliminated tasks which need not be done, you should rank those which need to be undertaken. These should be done with the following as yardsticks of merit.

—Rank highest those tasks that produce the most results per unit of effort.
—Pick future oriented tasks against past oriented ones.
—Select opportunity tasks rather than problem solving ones.
—Select tasks that aim high and will make a difference, rather than those that are safe and easy to do.

Remember, it is more productive to convert an opportunity into results than to solve a problem which restores the balance of the past. Problems which need to be solved should certainly be tackled, but should *not* be given priority over tasks which will produce results in the future. When this is not done, the role of a manager becomes mainly that of a problem solver and a maintainer of the working status quo. Such activity does not result in excellence of performance. The manager is left behind dealing with the past and the present. The future slips by him unnoticed.

Research studies in managerial competence have shown that excellence in achievement depends less on technical ability or managerial know how than on the courage to go after opportunity. Thus, it is courageous to go after opportunity rather than intelligent analysis, which should be the key to setting your priorities in tasks. This is the only way to get out of mediocrity and achieve managerial excellence.

The manager of sales coordination for a sewing machine factory, Barry N., was well respected for his ability to handle problems. He had become well versed in dealing with product allocation, supply demand mismatch, product scheduling, export shipping, customer claims and inland freight problems. It was hard work to tackle the multitude of problems which crept up daily and still keep the products moving to desired locations. There seemed to be no end to the work which needed to be done everyday. So it was with glee that he transferred this work to Wallace L., a young manager in the production plant, and accepted an equivalent staff position. The new manager of sales coordination saw tremendous opportunities for results in his new assignment. Wallace realized that problem solving was important, but relegated it in comparison to the opportunities he saw for results. He concentrated his efforts on inland freight reductions, increasing export revenues, realizing pending freight claims and following up on various cost reduction opportunities. Because of this, Wallace delegated problem solving activity to his section heads, who consulted him only for problems they couldn't handle themselves. This resulted in excellent performance of the sales coordination department. The young manager generated freight and cost reduction savings to unexpected proportions. Additional revenues from increased exports and freight claims improved the operating results of the whole organization. Within a year, Wallace was given additional responsibility and authority in the commercial operations of the organization, and his salary was more than doubled. He had risen from mediocrity to excellence, and was earmarked as top management material. This was in large measure because he had the courage to go after opportunities, rather than let himself be bogged down with problem solving.

To achieve excellence in your own work environment, you must decide what really matters and comes first in terms of opportunities. You must become the master of time and events, rather than be dictated by problem solving and other work pressures.

Priorities must be reconsidered and revised in the light of realities. As soon as you accomplish your priority tasks, the priorities of the other tasks before you change and should be revised.

Thus, prioritizing the opportunities before your work group should be a continuous activity. This is necessary if you want outstanding results from your own self and your people.

MAKING MEETINGS EFFECTIVE

A large portion of every manager's time is spent in meetings, reports or presentations—whether with individuals or with groups. For getting best results from others, it is necessary to make such meetings effective.

There are various common sense rules for making group meetings productive. Some of these are:

1. *Plan ahead for the meeting.* Ask for agenda items and/or distribute agenda well in time for others to come adequately prepared for the meeting. Ask people to take specific actions beforehand, such as preparing statistics, interviewing several employees to get reactions on a proposal, etc., whenever necessary.

2. *Guide the meeting on constructive channels.* Avoid it from becoming a battlefield for rivals. Also, do not permit time wasting digressions.

3. *Keep the atmosphere for discussion open.* Encourage people who generally remain quiet to have their say. Relieve tension with a joke or a pleasant story.

4. *Have someone note down the important points.* The attempt should be to record all important suggestions, agreements and action plans. Descriptions of how the discussions went are not necessary for working meetings.

5. *Take time to summarize and outline what needs to be done next.* Before the scheduled finish of the meeting, make sure that you summarize the main points and outline what needs to be done next.

6. *Assure follow-up.* Make sure that either your secretary, assistant, or you yourself send out a list of tasks to be done as a result of the meeting, with names of corresponding individuals responsible for implementation or follow-up. Give dates, wherever desirable and practical, by which these tasks should be done.

Managers can add to the above working guidelines to suit their own styles and situations. Nevertheless, the most indispensable point in making meetings effective is to clearly define in your own mind and to others its purpose and specific contribution.

Effective managers have a habit of insisting that the purpose be thought through and spelled out before a meeting is called, a report asked for or a presentation organized. Then they insist that the meeting serve the contribution to which it has been committed.

Focusing on contribution encourages relevance of events and teamwork. It helps to overcome the temptation to be preoccupied with efforts, work relationships, problems, weaknesses, etc., and gets the work group to concentrate on their fundamental commitment to generating results.

Thus, the basic ingredient which you need to use in dealing with meetings, reports and presentations is emphasis on contribution. Determine what contribution is desired, and focus on it to make all your meetings get you the results you want from your people.

GETTING TOUGH WHERE NECESSARY

In getting optimum results from people, a manager needs to have a feel for when to use democratic or participative leadership, and for when to be tough and autocratic.

The most desirable approach, of course, depends upon the situation. In general, as a manager you should be both autocratic and democratic in different situations.

In dealing with people, you will generally be faced with one of the following five situations. In each situation, the desirable behavior which you may plan to project has been spelled out:

1. *Information Collecting.* These situations cover interviewing new employees, getting staff member reports, hearing union grievances, etc. The recommended behavior here is participative. You have to get the facts out from others and get them to air their thoughts. Encourage others to speak out, and be flexible in your reactions. Do not impose your thoughts or actions on others in this situation.

2. *Information Giving.* This includes situations such as addressing an employee group, explaining a directive to your group, presenting a year end report, etc. The behavior here should be autocratic. The information flow is from you to others, so participative reactions are not in need here. You may accept suggestions, but in this situation you should be prepared to be firm or "tough" once a decision has been made.

3. *Decision Making.* Situations covered here are planning a cost reduction program, setting up a work schedule, establishing a new pricing policy, etc. The behavior style here should be participative. Every member of the group can contribute in making it a better decision. Also, participation of employees creates a commitment on their part for follow-up action, which is desirable. However, the conditions for participative management must exist, otherwise you will need to be autocratic and tough. [2]

4. *Problem Solving.* This includes solving customer problems, solving work flow breakdowns, handling urgent situations or crises, etc. Your behavior here should encourage participation. This is necessary in order to use all the resources available for achieving the best results.

5. *Decision Selling.* These situations cover getting employees to accept new organizational setups passed down by the board of directors, implementing changes in accounting practice, following up on decisions already made with the help of your work group, etc. Your behavior here needs to be autocratic. You cannot afford distractions or delays. Firmness, and even toughness in such situations would be appreciated by the majority of your work group. You may switch to participative leadership for carrying out the decisions, because individual contributions and suggestions can be helpful at such a stage. However, any attempts by a small

---

[2] These conditions have been listed in Chapter 10 under the section "How to Discuss Coming Changes in Groups."

segment of the work group to change a decision already made should be met with toughness.

Managers who have been firm and tough in their commitments have always gained results as well as employee admiration. You therefore need to be prepared to get tough where necessary in order to get the best results from your people.

Chapter 7

HOW TO HELP THOSE IN HIGHER RANKS TO HELP YOU

Every manager attempts to consciously manage subordinates. Very few managers, however, have learned how to effectively deal with those in higher ranks. Generally speaking, the approach is to consider oneself fortunate if one has a "good" boss, and unlucky if one has a "tough" or "unfair" individual as a boss. The tendency is for a manager to accept things from the above as something over which he has very little control. Nevertheless, effective managers have long learned that this is not true. People at the top can be made to respond in a positive manner. As a manager, you can get those in higher ranks to help you achieve success. It is suggested that you formulate your own strategy of how to deal with your boss and those in higher ranks, basing your strategy on the examples and clear cut guidelines presented in the following pages. Such a strategy is necessary to increase your overall effectiveness and success as a manager.

CULTIVATING YOUR BOSS

Contrary to popular misconceptions, individuals do not, as a rule, rise to position and prominence over the fallen bodies of incompetent bosses. In fact, if their boss is not promoted, subordinates will tend to be bottled up behind him. And if the boss is dismissed for incompetence or failure, the successor is rarely the young man next in line. He is usually brought in from the outside, often bringing his own bright young men with him. On the other hand, there is nothing quite as conducive to success as a successful and rapidly promoted boss.

The best strategy in dealing with your boss would be the one aimed at making his strengths productive. This is also the key to your own effectiveness. It will enable you to focus on your contribution in such a way that it finds receptivity upstairs and can be put to use. You will be able to achieve and accomplish the things which are relevant and important in your present situation.

How can you make the strengths of your boss productive?

One does not make the strengths of the boss productive by waiting on him hand and foot, or by being servile, or by bobbing one's head in rhythm every time he speaks. One can make strengths productive by first analyzing them. The effective manager accepts that his boss is human, i.e., has his strengths and also his limitations. He therefore asks questions such as "What can my boss do really well?" "What has he done really well in the past?" "What can I do to help him to perform better?" "What does he need to know to utilize his strengths fully?" He does not try to work on the weaknesses of the boss, but rather his main thrust is to support and help maximize the strengths of the boss. He counterbalances weak areas as much as possible without showing his boss up. It is not a good idea to try and "reform" the boss. This tendency is particularly strong in experienced subordinates who see themselves as the tutors to a newly appointed boss from the outside. Instead of trying to get their boss to overcome his limitations, the effective ones ask instead, "What can the new boss do well?" They then go on to optimize the functional areas in which the boss is strong. This maximizes performance and results by making strengths productive.

The effective manager looks for the ways, manners and habits which aid the performance of his boss. Some bosses only listen after they have read a note on a report. They are primarily readers. To others, it is a waste of time to submit a voluminous report, as they can only grasp what it is all about through the spoken word. They are primarily listeners. People who are both listeners and readers are rare. Effective individuals analyze, understand and follow the manner in which their boss works best. Some individuals like to have things summed up for them in one page. Others like to see pages and pages of figures on everything. Some want to be informed right from the early stages. Others do not want to hear about an idea or a subject until it is "ripe" for action. Let us see how a successful manager made the strengths of a boss he did not like productive, and thereby benefits himself.

> The new general manager, Harold C., was a tough man to get along with. He was given to short bursts of temper, had a tendency to pass the buck, and believed in favoring subordinates who were loyal members of his own informal group. Morgan S., the young administration manager, was a little wary about how he would fare under his new boss. Morgan, however, had learned early in his business experience to keep personal likes and dislikes out of working relationships as much as possible. He was all too aware of the glaring weaknesses of his new boss. He looked for strong areas and found Harold to be a sound production manager who could relate better than most people with the production worker. Morgan also found him strong in labor relations, cost reduction implementation, and design and development activity. Morgan concentrated on these activities, and worked closely with Harold in two major areas—increasing production and implementing cost reduction drives. Within a year, the factory showed outstanding improvement in these areas. The general manager got a pay raise, and the administration manager was promoted to additional general manager of the factory. He still did not like the short tempered nature of his boss, but this was minimized and overshadowed by their working together successfully on the strong areas of his boss. A few months after his promotion, Morgan was transferred to another factory in the same organization to head its operations as general manager.

All of us are experts on other people. We can see them much more clearly than they see themselves. To make one's boss effective can therefore be fairly easy. It simply requires cultivating and focusing on his strengths and what he can do. It requires building on strengths to make weaknesses irrelevant. Considerable experience has shown that few things can contribute as much to your effectiveness and success as building on the strengths of your boss.

LEARNING FROM YOUR BOSS

There are four ways in which you can learn from your boss.

1. *Concentrate and work with his strengths.* Naturally, your boss is likely to be most knowledgeable in the areas he is strong in and

has had past success. By working with him in these areas, you will be able to improve your own level of expertise and effectiveness, in addition to providing a contribution which he is likely to appreciate very much.

2. *Analyze and learn what you need to know to move into his job.* Strengthen the capabilities and knowledge you need to do the job of your boss effectively, so that you will be ready when such a need arises. A lot of managers do not take this effort in time, thereby making it necessary for someone else to be brought in to replace their boss if he leaves or has to be transferred suddenly. It is, therefore, a good idea to learn from your boss about all his contribution areas, rather than remain proficient in only the areas you are responsible for. This may require extra efforts and initiative on your part. These efforts and initiative are a good investment for future dividends, as they will keep you poised for any opportunity that may arise.

3. *Discuss organizational issues with him.* Keep a focus on the totality of the situation you are in. Avoid the tendency to be wrapped up only in your areas of activity. Discuss policy and broader organizational issues to always keep a clear picture of how the total organization functions, and how your activities influence and affect overall organizational objectives. Participate in organizational analysis with your boss pertaining to your own activities, and their co-relation to the achievement of organizational objectives. This will assist you to improve your own contributions by making them more relevant where necessary, and will enable you to learn from your boss about the responsibilities of higher management.

4. *Request more periodic feedback on yourself.* The best way to know what your boss thinks of you is to ask him. Don't assume what he must be thinking of you. Some people who thought that they got along fine with their bosses have been known to be dismissed or passed over for promotion. Others who had the impression that their bosses were not entirely pleased with them have often been surprised to get high raises and promotions. In others words, what your boss really thinks of you may not be clear at all in his interactions with you. Try and get feedback from him continuously on where you feel you can improve. This will not be to your disadvantage, but will provide you with a means to learn and

develop yourself to standards of excellence with the help of those in higher ranks. Let us see how a manager learned this lesson the hard way.

Roy K., the sales officer in charge of tools and castings in an engineering factory, was a very hard working individual. He got along well with his boss, Warren O., the marketing manager. He was also very highly regarded on a personal level by other senior officers because of his long association with the company. Nevertheless, he had been holding the same position for seven years with only mandatory pay increases, whereas others who had joined the company with him were holding ranks of either senior department managers or were general managers of other production plants. Roy knew that he followed instructions well, was well liked and worked hard. What he couldn't understand was why he was not being promoted and given more responsibility, authority and salary.

Roy's opportunity to develop came during a reorganization. He was transferred laterally as a sales officer to work directly under the general manager of the plant. There, Roy decided not to take a chance on appearances, and made it a habit to get feedback on how he could improve his contribution to the organization and qualify for promotions. His boss, Arnold F., started working closely with Roy to develop him into senior management potential. Since Roy opened his mind to get feedback, he realized that his failings in the area of new ideas, effective interdepartmental coordination, and knowledge of the company's total operations had kept him from rising to higher positions. He had thought that going along with past practices, and what was suggested from the top, was in his best interest. He was surely liked by those in higher ranks for being a good follower, but that was about all. No one thought Roy capable of strong leadership. He shied away from innovative needs and opportunities necessary to meet the changes which were occurring in the business environment constantly. So though everyone liked him since he tried to do what he was told, no one thought very highly of him. Arnold pointed this out to Roy when Roy asked for his feedback.

Being made aware of how he could change his approach to the job to demonstrate his innovativeness and leadership ability, Roy concentrated the next six months in these areas. He thought of new ideas to increase sales efficiency, made recommendations for improving sales production planning to increase the coordination of different departments, and kept the needs and objectives of the total division in mind while implementing his department's functions. He improved his department's performance dramatically by not being afraid to implement desirable changes and new ideas. He had risen from a level of mediocrity to one of excellence with the assistance of the feedback from his boss.

Do not take for granted that those in higher ranks will provide you with all the necessary feedback for your development on their own. You have to help them to help you. Ask them about any areas where your personal performance could be improved. This will make it easier for them to frankly discuss and point out what they consider important. By getting such a feedback you will be able to concentrate on areas which are relevant to your progress in the organization. The mere action of discussing your development with those in higher ranks creates a favorable impression and helps establish a personal rapport.

Some individuals tend to think that by asking for feedback on how they can improve their performance they are acknowledging that their performance is unsatisfactory. Every individual can bear personal improvement. By asking for feedback to further improve oneself, an individual is demonstrating a very appreciable characteristic and an important one for success—a zest for self-development. Those in higher ranks appreciate such a zest, particularly when this is approached with sincerity and confidence. Do not hesitate, therefore, to ask for feedback from your superiors. This is one of the best ways to help them to help you.

DEALING WITH OTHERS IN UPPER RANKS

There are three aspects of dealing with those in upper ranks which are particularly important.

1. *Do not join any clique or group.* Most organizations have management cliques. Generally speaking, a manager has to align himself with one of two or more informal groups. It is very advantageous to remain non-aligned. Do not avoid any person or group. Share activities and interests with each of the cliques or groups without committing yourself in any way. This is not as difficult to do as it may appear, but does require individuality as well as capability on your part. Sometimes this may not be possible. In other words, despite your best efforts, a certain organizational

group may reject you out of jealousy, misunderstanding or purely selfish reasons. Under such circumstances, make it a point not to antagonize or criticize that group—remain non-committal. Criticism which is not purely constructive or asked for never pays in any organization or social group. Let us see how one manager approached organizational non-alignment.

The air conditioning manufacturing plant had two management factions. One was headed by Lawrence J., the general manager, and the other by the production manager, Buddy M., who was senior in service to the general manager. Some departmental managers were clearly in Lawrence's group, and quite a few others formed Buddy's group. The production manager couldn't be changed, as most of the production engineers and assistant managers belonged to his group, giving him tremendous power in the organization.

The last industrial relations manager had committed the folly of joining the general manager group. He received so little cooperation from the production department that he couldn't function effectively, and had to be dismissed from service by the director in charge of the plant. The new industrial relations manager, Bruce R., realized that it was best for him to avoid aligning himself with any group. He criticized no one, avoided back biting and remained above factional disputes. Nevertheless, he developed personal contacts with members of both groups. In due time, both groups recognized Bruce as neutral but friendly. They accepted him as such after he politely maintained his neutrality despite pressures from both sides. When an opportunity came up for Bruce to be promoted to the position of commercial manager, neither of the groups opposed it—in fact, he continued to get cooperation from both factions.

It does require courage and confidence to remain neutral in organizational politics. It has, however, been found that consistent neutrality has always won admiration and help from all factions concerned.

2. *Be polite and interested but not obsequious.* Some individuals may think that the best way to deal with those in higher ranks is to be extremely complimentary, to jump at their very command and, in general, fawn over them in order to please them continuously. Experience has shown otherwise. Some senior people like flattery and being attended to hand and foot, but do not think very highly of individuals who provide them with this pleasure. Others are

turned off by continuous flattery and servility. In any situation, the best way to deal with people in higher ranks is through politeness and interest. Normal courtesy to individuals and interest in their work makes them appreciative of you. They then develop mutual rapport and attempt to help you when they can.

3. *Be frank in your dealings.* Quite often, one finds that after working in an organization, there are some people in higher ranks who like you, others who are lukewarm, and sometimes there are one or more who are clearly hostile. It is a good idea to try and find out why some of the superiors are hostile, if such a situation exists. You can attempt to discover this by self-analysis—review your dealings and interactions to see what could have caused hostility to arise. After pinpointing the possible reason, try to correct it and see if it makes a difference. If it does not, or if you are not sure of the cause of the hostility, it is best to have a frank chat with the person or persons concerned individually. Don't mince words. It is beneficial to express at the outset that you want to maintain good working relationships, and if there is any area which needs improvement, you would be glad to hear about it and try to improve it. This generally opens up people, and they will bring out what has been bothering them. Very often, this may only be a simple misunderstanding which can be easily explained or clarified, sometimes it may be something which will require greater effort on your part to handle. Whatever it is, it will help to clear the air and set the stage for improved working relationships. This approach will help others to express themselves frankly to assist you in improving your effectiveness.

> Albert E., the young administrative manager, who had been transferred from the head office to the factory, could not understand why he was not liked by his new boss, Paul T., the plant general manager. On various instances, Al was put on the spot by Paul's criticism. This went on to such an extent that Al asked for a transfer to the corporate head office for a staff position, which he was fortunate in getting. Before leaving, he asked Paul, for whom he had worked for two years, why he did not like him. The general manager told him frankly that he was irked by the voluminous reports and paperwork the administrative manager generated, which Paul felt caused more problems than they solved. Had Al asked this earlier, he could have changed his working style, made his reports shorter, and produced them only when necessary after preliminary

discussion with the general manager. It was such a simple matter—making reports *for* discussion or *after* discussion. He thought the former was the way, whereas his boss was irked by it and preferred the latter approach. He found this out too late to change the black mark of an unsuccessful assignment at the plant level.

As soon as one senses hostility from people in higher ranks, it is a good idea to discuss it frankly in order to remove its root cause. Managers who avoid to do this early, find that it is not much use doing it after its ill consequences have already taken place. Nevertheless, when done in time it prompts those in higher ranks to cooperate in improving working relationships.

By dealing with others in upper ranks according to the preceding three guidelines, you will help those in higher ranks to help you.

SECRETS OF SELLING YOUR IDEAS

We have already discussed in chapter four the basic technique to be used in selling your ideas successfully. It consists of the following steps.

Step 1. State at the outset the most significant benefits of your idea—stress benefits—not features. In professional terms, this is often called making an initial benefit statement.

Step 2. Probe for specific interests and needs and relate them to your idea.

Step 3. Answer objections.

Step 4. Summarize agreed to benefits and ask for an acceptance/commitment to the idea.

Step 5. Discuss follow through for implementation.

The above is a tested successful approach to selling used by organizations such as Xerox Corporation, IBM, etc.[1] This approach also forms the basis of developing professional selling skills at different levels of the organization through sales development seminars, sales force training programs and executive development programs. To instill this systematic approach to selling, role play situations are often used.

---

[1] For a detailed discussion of each step, please see Chapter 4.

When you have a selling situation—whether it is selling an idea, a program, an investment or whatever, rehearse this approach before making the actual sales presentation. Determine how you are going to introduce the idea or item, and to what needs of the listener you are going to relate the benefits from your idea in your opening initial benefit statement. Once you have figured this out, your idea will be easier to sell as people buy benefits and not anything else. When someone buys a home refrigerator, it is for the benefit of storing perishables, keeping beverages cold, getting ice for household usage, etc. in an efficient and economical manner. He is not interested in buying a compressor, a cabinet, and a refrigeration system in itself—but for what it can do and what it signifies. Therefore, relating to benefits or how something will best meet existing needs is crucial—technical or functional details in themselves are secondary. They have meaning only when associated with the benefits they provide.

After the initial benefit statement, plan on probing for specific interests and actual needs. Rehearse what questions you are going to ask to make the probing effective. Once you have obtained agreement or commitment on needs, relate the benefits of your idea or item to them. Explain how your idea will satisfy existing needs and, where possible, future needs as well.

In all probability, you are bound to receive a major objection to your idea in some form or the other. It is necessary therefore to anticipate what some of the major objections may be and develop replies to overcome them.

After the objections have been answered,[2] plan to take the first opportunity to summarize the benefits agreed to by the listener and ask for acceptance of the idea. If accepted, plan to discuss then how it would be followed up for implementation. If it is not accepted, find out the objection and answer it. Again, summarize all the agreed to benefits and ask for acceptance.

The above five step approach to selling has to be adjusted and polished to meet each situation and the personality of the listener. The more you follow the sequence and logic of the five steps, the greater will be your effectiveness in selling ideas.

The following practical hints will further assist in selling your ideas.

---

[2] In Chapter 4, see section on "Selling Your Own Ideas to Achieve Creative Action," Step 3, for a suggested approach to effective handling of objections.

1. *Emotions persuade more effectively than facts.* You must have facts, of course, but an emotional catalyst will help to put them across better. Relate facts to existing conditions, needs and emotions, and stress their impact rather than leave that to the imagination of the listener.

2. *Take your time.* Even intelligent people have trouble with new ideas. Sometimes new or somewhat complicated concepts take time to get accepted. You may need to sell them for a considerable period, bit by bit, repeating your message in as many different ways as you can. In your discussions, try to cover anticipated objections before they are actually voiced. Furthermore, give your theme new interest every time you present it.

> A factory manager, Jerry A., was getting concerned about the safety record of his plant. He had been trying to sell the idea for new and improved safety equipment to the director of manufacturing for some time. The director seemed to think that the high accident rate was due to employee carelessness. Therefore, he was reluctant to sanction a significant amount to be spent on new safety equipment. Jerry decided to try a new approach. He wrote to the national safety council, which forwarded data on the new safety equipment and its tested improvements in preventing accidents. To counteract the element of employee carelessness, he circulated current newspaper clippings about industrial accidents, and compiled a scrapbook of many authenticated cases where carelessness on the job had led to injury or death. Being satisfied that employee carelessness was being tackled systematically by Jerry, and having seen supporting data on the new safety equipment, the director of manufacturing agreed to have the new equipment installed on a trial basis. The accident record fell dramatically in the next three months, and productivity increased significantly. Jerry proved his point that the improved safety equipment would more than pay for itself in terms of higher productivity and increased employee morale—by enthusiastically trying out a new approach.

If acceptance of your idea takes time, keep following it up with as many new approaches as possible. If you yourself are convinced of its benefits, it is only a matter of time and enthusiastic follow-up before its benefits are understood and it is accepted.

3. *Stress personal involvement.* An idea is best understood if the listeners are allowed to picture themselves as being direct beneficiaries of its implementation. To do this, present the idea

from the point of view of the listeners, involving them as much as possible through all the stages of the idea. Ask for and incorporate their viewpoints, needs, interests and priorities, and then relate your idea to them.

4. *Determine the best time for your proposal.* Ask yourself questions such as: "Will the idea, if accepted, avoid conflict with other projects already underway?" "Can the idea be implemented now if those in higher ranks accept it?" "Is the idea fully developed?" If the answer to these questions is yes, your idea is probably ripe for presentation. By preparing for its presentation on the basis of the five step approach outlined earlier, you will greatly increase the chances of your idea being accepted.

It has been seen that good ideas do not sell themselves. The secret is in knowing how to sell them. The simple approach outlined in this chapter will help you to do just that.

Chapter 8

HOW TO ACCOMPLISH MORE THROUGH OTHERS

Every manager faces the situation when he wishes that he could have done more on a particular day. The more dynamic and capable an individual, the more he tends to accomplish. Some managers, particularly those swamped with responsibility, wish there was more time to do things. This is wishful thinking, as time is a limited resource. It cannot be increased or decreased. It has a fixed and uniform rate of passage. The variable is how much can be accomplished in units of time. Every manager's effectiveness depends upon how well he can control this variable. Thus, the ability to accomplish more through others distinguishes the successful manager from others who cannot efficiently handle the deluge of managerial work.

OVERCOMING EVERY MANAGER'S PROBLEM—TOO MANY THINGS TO DO

Experience has shown that effective managers plan their work and work their plan. They do not let themselves be led from one problem to another. They give priority to opportunities as well as problems that will impact the future, and discard problems of the past. Most importantly, they plan to devote a large measure of their time on realizing opportunities and generating results—not on handling problems. They can do this only because they stress "planning," the single most important activity for any manager.

Let us take a look at how one successful manager planned his work to overcome the problems of too many things to do.

Murray L., the marketing manager of a large durable consumer product, put in long hours every day to meet the demands for so many things to be accomplished on an urgent basis.

But he found that despite his long hours, he was using most of his time solving distribution, product scheduling and pricing problems. Murray had very little time left for productive work to improve sales and marketing efficiencies. Nor could he keep abreast of what was happening in the market in terms of consumer preferences, competitive activity and new opportunities. He knew that he had to do something to have more time for product innovation, sales promotion and market analysis activities. He felt that he should get an assistant marketing manager to share the work load, but there was a hiring freeze in the company, and he knew that he would have to look elsewhere for a solution.

Murray decided to do some self-analysis and get all the books he could on executive effectiveness to see where improvements could be made. He also studied and discussed the work planning of other successful executives and arrived at the following approach to his own work planning.

First, he learned that it was important to make a *list* of the opportunities (or immediate result objectives) and problems facing him and his part of the organization. He then gave priority to the opportunities and problems. He crossed out problems which had no significant impact on the future and selected those that were necessary to be attended to as they impacted on the result areas. Some of these problems, such as claims with freight companies, procedure complaints, outstanding payments, etc., Murray either wrote off or delegated to appropriate section heads. Then he planned his work on a monthly basis for a quarter and on a *daily* basis for the current month. He analyzed his own work pattern and kept the morning (his most efficient time) for major opportunities and one or two crucial problems. Two afternoons a week he kept for routine work and other problems. He kept other afternoons free for what might come up, meetings, and for following up on opportunities.

Murray learned that while planning his work it was advantageous to schedule unpleasant tasks *as early as possible.* By doing these first he would not worry about them all the time. This made him feel lighter, more confident, and he enjoyed his work more. In his work planning, Murray allowed sufficient time every week for following up on major tasks. By planning his work schedule on a realistic basis, he continuously found that his efficiency soared, and he got the satisfaction which comes with doing a job well.

From the above instance, it is clear that you can overcome the problem of too many things to do if you follow a systematic approach to work planning. This can be implemented in the following four steps.

Step 1. Planning effectively. List all the opportunities and problems which face you. Spread these out on a priority basis over a 3 month period. Then plan on a *daily* basis for the current month. Emphasize opportunities over problems. Make this a continuous exercise at the end of every month.

Step 2. Working efficiently. Fit your daily work schedule according to your own energy patterns during the day, keeping the best time for opportunities or crucial problems, and your slow period for all other work. Plan to do unpleasant and difficult tasks without delay to avoid worrying about them. This will help you to concentrate fully on other important tasks with an unburdened mind. It is important that you enjoy your work, so plan your daily schedule so that you will look forward to it.

Step 3. Delegating as much as possible. While you are dealing with opportunities and problems, delegate tasks to different individuals or groups if (1) you think they are capable of carrying out the assignment without assistance or (2) if you think that they will develop individually in carrying out the assignment under your supervision. In other words, do not hesitate to use delegation as a tool to accomplish more through others as well as to develop subordinates.

Both at the work planning and implementation stage delegate tasks to be done as much as possible. [1]

Step 4 Following up. The other three steps will bear fruit only when you follow up on them. It is best to include follow-up activities in your work schedule. This should cover a periodic review of your plan (weekly or monthly as the situation demands). Following up on opportunities, crucial problems and delegated tasks should not be left in the air, but should be specifically put on your work diary so that it is not missed or approached when it is too late.

---

[1] For a working approach on when and how to delegate, please see section on "How to Delegate Tasks to Be Done" in Chapter 3.

These four steps form the basis of scheduling managerial work load in a practical manner to accomplish more through others. Much of the success of this will depend upon your subordinates. It is therefore in your best interests to continuously develop your subordinates.

STARTING THE DEVELOPMENT OF YOUR SUBORDINATES

Your success lies in how well you can get your work team to perform. In order to accomplish work objectives it is not only necessary to motivate employees, but also to develop them to meet existing and future organizational needs.

The first step in starting the development of your subordinates is to think through what each man under you is capable of doing. To be able to do this, you have to systematically appraise each individual. There is no standard appraisal or merit rating form. The best approach is to make a list of the qualities and performance criteria most relevant to your organizational environment. Some of the important attributes which successful employee appraisals should cover are:

1. Ability to achieve assigned goals and complete assignments.
2. Use of imagination and the ability to devise better ways of doing things.
3. Ability to get thoughts and ideas across clearly and effectively.
4. Knack of dealing with people; understanding how individuals react and getting them to work well together.
5. Healthy ambition.
6. Willingness to profit from constructive criticisms.

You could rank each attribute or criteria on a scale of 1 to 5 or 1 to 10 for each individual employee.[2] In this way, you will have an analysis of the strengths and weaknesses of your subordinates individually. Individual appraisal will help to answer two key questions in the development of each subordinate.

1. Is the employee placed in the job where he can make the greatest contribution to the organization?
2. What weaknesses does he have to overcome, and what does he have to learn to fully realize his strengths and capacities?

---

[2] For a review of various merit rating systems, see Prentice-Hall, Inc., *Personnel Policies and Practices.*

The answers to the above two questions will decide what specific action needs to be taken to initiate and promote employee development. It may mean a change in job assignment, special training, or assignment of group or individual projects to encourage leadership and teamwork, etc.

In any event, it is important that you review, with each of your subordinates, his personal appraisal to bring out and suggest areas for improvement and self-development. This step is the key to initiating the development of your subordinates. Feedback from you as to how they are doing and where they can improve their performance and individual capabilities will encourage and motivate your people to develop themselves. Let us see how this approach can be implemented successfully.

> A new accounts manager improved the working efficiency of a poorly performing accounts department by reviewing with each subordinate how he could develop himself individually and improve departmental performance. After just one month's observation and judgement of performance records, he reviewed each employee's developmental needs and aspirations. He took the suggestions made by some employees in these sessions as valid, and implemented them to improve existing work flows. He changed the assignments of three section heads after an analysis of their strengths, weaknesses and interests. These individual reviews had amazing motivational impact. People wanted to perform better, and showed individual prowess and progress. They knew that their progress would be closely watched, and that performance improvements would be appreciated and rewarded. The accounts manager found that starting the development of his new subordinates had a significant motivating effect. It helped his people to improve their working efficiency by taking a greater interest in their jobs. It improved his people's personal traits, and this resulted in a more satisfactory performance on their part.

To maintain the impetus generated by these review sessions, it is advantageous to delegate independent assignments which give a good measure of responsibility and authority to promising subordinates. Nothing develops an individual faster than the responsibility to perform a little beyond his normal reach. You can use this approach by giving challenging assignments to different subordinates in the areas of their strengths and interests, so that they gain both confidence and broader experience.

It is important to try and develop each individual employee—

including top, average and low performers. Unlike what some people may tend to think, a manager should not concentrate mainly on developing poor performers, or problem people, into productive individuals. It is no less important to develop top performers into even better performers, as they need less time and effort to be motivated. Furthermore, a 10% improvement in the performance of top performers means a far greater impact than a 10% improvement in the low performers.

Group dynamics is a new approach to employee development which has been found to be very successful. It can be used to complement the individual counselling approach discussed above. The form of training involving group dynamics is called T-group or training group, also referred to sometimes as sensitivity training. The purpose is to allow an employee to see himself at work as others see him. The general method used in an organizational environment has already been discussed. [3] The T-group procedure can be used to develop members of any group. Such a group may consist entirely of peers, or of people at different levels in the organizational family, such as a manager and his subordinates. This new approach provides a tremendous tool to start the development of individuals in any work group. It makes people aware of how they come across to other people, and what their strengths and weaknesses are as viewed by others. The mere knowledge of this, when discussed in a group environment, guides individuals effectively in their own self-development. It also helps in understanding and appreciating the forces that come into play in a work group situation. One is made more sensitive to the social and emotional needs of the work group and its individual members. This sensitivity helps to develop individuals, and gives power, resilience and effectiveness to work groups.

The following four step approach is the gist of the preceding discussion. These four steps will help you to develop your subordinates, both individually and organizationally.

> *Step 1.* - Appraise each individual member of your work group.
> *Step 2.* - Hold individual counselling sessions to discuss where each employee stands.
> *Step 3.* - Provide opportunities for independent assignments,

---

[3] Please see the section titled "Using sensitivity training to improve relationships" in Chapter 4.

projects, studies, etc. to feed the initiative and potential assessed in different individuals.

Step 4. - Aim at the overall development of the work group through T-group sessions.

It is best to follow these four steps in the sequence they have been presented. This approach will develop your subordinates individually and as a group to assist you in accomplishing common work objectives in an effective and efficient manner.

ALLOCATING ROUTINE WORK EFFICIENTLY

An important means of accomplishing more through others is to allocate routine work efficiently. When should routine work be allocated? How should it be allocated? How should it be organized? What is an efficient way of following up? These are some of the major questions we shall cover here.

There are many managers who are swamped with work from a number of areas at the same time. They have, therefore, developed an approach of handling problems as they come, and with whatever time is left, they try to run their departments or organizations efficiently. Unfortunately, they find that problem solving takes so much time that little is available for anything else. Therefore, every manager must develop an efficient approach to handling routine work with minimum time expense, and yet maintain an excellent level of performance.

Studies of successful managers have shown that for optimum performance you should approach your work load in the following manner.

I. *Give priority to opportunities over problems.*

Results exist in the present and the future. Focussing on opportunities or future oriented objectives will help you to get results. The past is a part of history. All problems are steeped in the past. Only those problems which will significantly *impact the future* are worth tackling. This is certainly not implying that you neglect or forget past issues, but only means that they be tackled in the proper perspective. Give first priority to opportunities or tasks that will produce results. If an issue or problem fits in this category, i.e., its solution will generate desirable results in the future, then include it in your top priority list. Tackle all other problems with minimal time expense as and when they crop up. A lot of old problems solve themselves over time and in the process of other result oriented activity.

A very successful sales executive was asked how he performed so well consistently. He illustrated how he got results by focussing on opportunities rather than problems. Before the start of every month in a small pocket planning diary, he made out a list of opportunities or result oriented activities that he would achieve. He also made out a list of urgent problems which he needed to address. These were problems which would impact the present and the future. He then allocated opportunities and problems on a daily basis for the month in his daily work diary. Even when attending to a problem, he sought out an opportunity or alternative to take care of the problem as well as future needs. For example, one of his clients was very upset with the performance of the equipment which he had leased. He was threatening to cancel the lease and return the equipment, as it was continuously breaking down. The sales executive analyzed the situation. He studied when the equipment was leased and what the work load was at that time. He found that the work load on the equipment had practically doubled and, in fact, the customer's needs had grown in other areas, too. He explained this to the customer and pointed out that the increased present work load, as well as future needs, could be met more reliably and at a lower per unit cost on a more capable type of equipment. When facts were presented to the customer, and examples of the new equipment's reliability cited, he agreed to lease the more capable new equipment. The lease rental of the new equipment was two and half times that of the old one, but it did in fact serve the increased needs of the customer better and at a lower per unit cost. The successful sales executive did not approach the situation as one of making the old equipment work satisfactorily. That would have been merely short term problem solving. He looked for future needs and opportunities in the problem situation, and suggested a suitable alternative which made the customer happy and got him more business.

Problems therefore should never be tackled in their past perspective. Present and future needs must be taken into account. Alternatives which will yield better performance or results and at the same time remove the problem should be proposed and implemented.

II. *Allocate routine tasks and ideas immediately.*
Very often we plan to allocate a task, make an inquiry, discuss

an assignment, or follow up on something with other people, but in the rush of something else, either forget about it or never get around to doing it. The higher the responsibility we have, the more we need to do such things and the less time we have to do them. Therefore, we need to develop an efficient system to do all of these things as soon as possible without forgetting about them or spending too much time, since we want to focus most of our time on opportunities and related problems. Many successful managers have developed such a system, which is one reason why they are successful. Let us see how one such manager implemented a system in his own particular situation to do all these things in an efficient manner, with the least expense of his time.

When the general manager of the head office of a large organization was fired, he was replaced by an individual renowned for his efficiency. The new general manager had risen to the rank of secretary/treasurer in a subsidiary company after joining it as a simple clerk. He had achieved this phenomenal advancement by continuously developing himself and improving his managerial abilities. One of the strengths he had developed was improving office and organizational efficiency. Though he had eight large departments reporting to him (including the time consuming publicity, personnel and accounting departments), he was able to run all of them efficiently and still spend most of his time on long term planning and organizational opportunities. He did this in a very simple manner—one which can be followed by every manager in his own particular situation. Every day he would set aside 15 minutes in the morning to write a slip of paper for each routine item to different subordinates. These slips of paper served to do things like allocate a task, ask for information, make an inquiry, provide information, introduce an idea, make a suggestion, or follow up on something which was overdue or pending. His secretary refilled the little box of these blank ordinary paper slips (4 1/4" x 5 1/2") on his desk, and distributed at least ten to fifteen of these slips every day. This took the least bit of time necessary to initiate and follow up on a number of things which were on his mind. The general manager would make a note on the more important of these slips specifying a time whereby he wanted a reply. He would also record for follow-up purposes the important items in his work diary, so that he could check them out in the coming few days. This helped to take the load off his mind in the morning for most of the small but necessary things which had to be done. He could then devote most of the time in the day for productive work scheduled in his work diary. During the busy schedule of his work day, whenever he got time, he would check out the replies to his slips, and write fresh ones for getting other things done which had cropped up in the meantime. Such slips kept communications between him and his subordinates effective all the time, so that when he had individual meetings with them, they were well prepared, and relevant discussions could be held. He encouraged his subordinates to use this system too, and to send him answers or feed new information to him through similar slips. This avoided the need for them to wait in order to see him, and helped to get things accomplished without any delays. These slips were the means of generating a lot of useful activity, and were followed up by individual meetings, formal authorizations, etc. wherever necessary. They served to increase overall effectiveness by allocating routine work efficiently. They reduced the need for the general manager to talk or meet with subordinates on every small issue, thereby giving him time for more productive work.

The above approach to accomplishing more through others can be followed by every manager in his own particular situation. For maximum effectiveness, it has become essential that every manager plan the coming month in a work diary on a daily or weekly basis, depending upon the nature of his work. Most successful managers follow this practice. To maximize the benefits of such a simple yet effective planning tool, it is necessary to follow the approach outlined above—focussing on opportunities and allocating routine work and ideas in the most convenient and effective manner. Nothing is simpler than the use of communication slips to help you in allocating routine work immediately and efficiently. The use of these simple tools—the work diary and communication slips—in the manner discussed will most certainly help you to increase your effectiveness directly in proportion to how well you use these tools.

FOLLOWING UP WITHOUT HARASSING

Following up is a useful activity if done without harassing. If the subordinates feel harassed, then the quality of work and their morale is likely to suffer. The following steps will help you to do your follow-up activity in an effective manner without the undesirable effect of harassing.

Step 1. Set Mutual Deadlines. When allocating tasks, set a deadline which is agreed to or accepted by the employee or the work group. This generates a commitment as to the completion time of the job or assignment. It thereby helps to make follow-up activity relevant. Contrary to what some may think, it does not pay in the long run to set deadlines simply to pressure employees into getting the job done within a few days after the deadline. It has been found that challenging deadlines which are achievable help to provide a sense of accomplishment which motivates employees to perform better.

Step 2. Understand Difficulties. If an assignment or job is going slowly, or has not been met on time, *first* find out why. Understand the problem which the individual or work group may be facing. If there is a genuine problem or need for assistance, provide the necessary support as far as practical. Incorporate valid suggestions from employees. Lend your assistance or advice as required. This will be very much appreciated and motivate the satisfactory completion of tough assignments.

Step 3. Set New Deadlines. When it becomes clear that due to unforeseen difficulties an assignment or job will not be completed as planned, reassess the situation and set new deadlines which are mutually acceptable.

Step 4. Send Appropriate Reminders. As an important part of your follow-up efforts, send a "communication" slip before the deadline to the concerned employee or work group for all important jobs. The time when this is to be done should be noted in your work diary. It is a good idea to plan on sending the reminder in the form of a query to the effect that you be informed of difficulties, if any, in getting the important assignment or job out in time. This ensures that problems are brought to the surface *when there is still time.* Rather than facing difficulties at the last minute, tackling them earlier often results in a simple resolution to get the job completed in time. A lot depends upon the timeliness and content of your reminders for getting important assignments completed within the established deadlines. On the spot visits should be made wherever possible, as they not only serve as reminders, but also help to solve problems immediately and motivate employees by your special attention.

This four step approach will help you to ensure that your people do not feel harassed when you follow up on important assignments with them.

DEVELOPING SUBORDINATES TOWARD LONG RANGE OBJECTIVES

Long term subordinate development cannot be just "promotion planning," confined to "promotable people," and geared to finding "back up men" for vacancies at successive levels. "Promotion planning" assumes that the job at successive levels, as well as the organizational structure, will remain unchanged so that one simply needs to develop people to fit into the shoes of today's total jobs. It is obvious, however, that both job requirements and organizational structure will change in the future, as they have always done in the past. So while planning on the development of your subordinates, plan on developing them to meet present *and* future needs. Thus the first principle of subordinate development is that it must be dynamic. It must always focus on the needs of tomorrow. It must cover what additional skills subordinates have to acquire, and what knowledge and ability they have to possess to meet the organizational needs of the future. The second principle of subordinate development is to develop the entire work group. To focus on the development of only a few promising individuals will yield minimal results. The people who need development the most are those who are not good enough to be promoted, but not bad enough to be fired. These constitute the majority in most work groups, and do the bulk of the actual work. Unless they are helped to grow along with the promising individuals, the whole work group will be inadequate. Furthermore, whatever could be gained by developing a chosen few would be more than offset by the resentment and frustration of those passed over.

Keeping the above principles in mind, the first step is to do "manpower planning." This covers the analysis of the future needs of your part of the organization and its objectives. This will help determine future organizational structure, decide what jobs will have to be filled, and determine what their requirements will be. Having determined to what capabilities you want to develop your subordinates, you can then take the following two steps to implement their development:

> *Step 1. Assess individual needs for development.* We have already discussed this earlier under "starting the development of your subordinates."
>
> *Step 2. Motivate self-development.* This can be done in a number of ways depending upon the development needs of an individual. It may be a move to another assignment. It may be formal schooling in management principles or in a specific subject. It may be a special assignment to handle a problem, or to study a proposed new procedure or program. The largest benefit comes from independent

assignments to prove one's worth. No individual should be made to do what he doesn't like doing. Individual needs can be taken care of in a small company by adjusting and changing the scope of a man's job. In larger organizations, the same effect can be achieved by transferring people to those jobs which best fit the development needs of the individual employees. These are, of course, very important decisions and must be fully participated in by the employee concerned. Sensitivity training or the "T-group" approach, as discussed earlier, is an excellent means of promoting both individual and work group development. The use of this development tool is rising, and it will become more and more significant in organizational group development as it is developed further. Another effective yet simple means of promoting employee self-development is through encouraging relevant reading in the areas of interest and need. A good reading list can cover much more than some time consuming training sessions do.

The key to subordinate long term development is that it has to be *self-development*. No business enterprise or manager is competent or really obligated to substitute its efforts for the self-development efforts of the employee. To do this would be mere foolish pretension. Nevertheless, every manager in a businss has the opportunity to encourage individual self-development or to stifle it, to direct it or to avoid it. Every manager must help all employees working with him to focus, direct and apply their self-development effort productively, if he wants to accomplish an increase in work productivity and success.

No one learns as much about a subject as the one who is forced to teach it. Similarly, no one develops as much as the manager who is trying to help others to develop themselves. In fact, no one can develop himself unless he works on the development of others. This is because it is in and through the efforts to develop others that you can raise the demand on yourself. The best performers in any profession, be it music, surgery or management, always look upon the people they have trained and developed as the proudest monuments they can leave behind.

ACCOMPLISHING WORK OBJECTIVES

Once your work objectives are set, you are faced with working through others to accomplish them. The better you can work with and through others, the more successful you will be in accomplishing these objectives.

In working through others, there are two things to keep in mind: (1) you must know whom to work with and how to work with them, and (2) you multiply your effectiveness many more times when you work with the right people in the right way.

Whether consciously or unconsciously, managers make a choice in using their discretionary time among the people they work with, from the top performers to the poorest performers. Some managers, without being aware of it, become involved in every matter that comes to their attention because someone writes them a letter, calls them on the telephone, knocks on their door or makes some other such demand on their time. Successful managers know whom to work with and how to use their time. In other words, they put their time to work for them, rather than letting random demands determine where and how their time will be deployed.

There is a difference between "being responsive to" and "becoming involved in" everything that comes to one's attention. This is a concept which is critical to the useful deployment of discretionary time. You may maintain an open door policy (letting everyone bring things to your attention) without becoming involved in every matter. Instead, you can use this opportunity to show others how to direct work into proper channels. In this way you can be responsive, without becoming involved, in the matters that are better handled by others.

A manager may hear others out and then go to work helping them solve their problem. Another manager may also hear them out, and then guide them to solve the problem themselves, or, where applicable, suggest the right person with whom the problem can be discussed and handled most effectively. While doing this, he explains why the problem should be discussed in greater detail with the suggested person rather than with himself. The first manager has let random demands determine how his time will be used; the second deploys his time on a discretionary basis, and yet is responsive without necessarily becoming involved.

Every manager should have an accurate idea of where his time goes. This is best done by keeping a time log himself, or by asking his secretary to keep one. This time log may be kept for a week or a month, depending upon how much the work pattern fluctuates during the week and from week to week. It should simply record the time spent with different people or alone by the manager, and should indicate the broad coverage of what was discussed or done during each time period. Such a time analysis never fails to surprise the manager concerned. Unless we consciously plan and regulate the use of our time, it is amazing how often we think we utilize our time well, when the facts show differently. Such a simple time analysis points out the time wasters, the random time stealers, and the activities (like some meetings) which can either be eliminated or reduced. Furthermore, such a time analysis will show you how much time you spend with your top performers, the mid-range performers and the poor performers. This knowledge is important in order to plan how you can improve your effectiveness in working with and through others.

Let us see how successful managers work with top, mid-range, and low-level producers to understand how best time may be deployed for full effectiveness.

Working with Top Performers: Should a manager spend any time with top performers? Some managers say that they never have to spend any time with their top men. Top performers usually know their job pretty well and don't ask for help. Other managers say that they only work through their top performers.

The manager who says he never spends any time with his top producers because they don't need his help is saying, in effect, that he doesn't understand effectiveness in working through people. For one thing, just a 10 percent increase in the effectiveness of top performers generates a far greater contribution to overall output than a 10 percent increase in the productivity of mid-range and poor performers. Therefore, any time taken up with increasing the productivity of top performers will yield a much greater return than the time spent with other employees. Furthermore, it is the function of every manager to help his subordinates to (1) do their present jobs better and (2) develop themselves for greater responsibility and more challenging assignments. Unless a manager is doing these things he is not working through others; he is simply letting others do the work. The following six step program is suggested:

1. *Keep top performers informed.* Top performers want to make things happen. This requires that they be kept informed about objectives, priorities, programs and constraints. This will help to channel their efforts productively into the achievement of desired work objectives.

2. *Help plan work programs.* Provide all the information needed by top performers to plan their individual work programs to achieve organizational objectives. Give specific guidelines and direction. Provide answers to questions such as what's wanted. How much? What pitfalls should be avoided? What additional resources and support is available, etc. Top performers work best when they don't have to waste time digging answers because they lack guidance and direction. Working on the plan together builds a commitment to put plans into action.

3. *Give top producers ample opportunity to talk about their ideas.* Good employees have good ideas, and top performers often have some of the best ideas. Subordinates want to talk out their ideas with someone who can help them see how these ideas might fit into the big picture. Employees gain greater confidence in their own ability to contribute when managers listen to what they say. Unfortunately, the opposite is also true. A sense of resentment arises when a manager won't take time to listen. Moreover, employees soon lose confidence in their ability to make contributions under such a supervisor. A major step in motivating top performers is to listen to their ideas, which often suggest better ways of accomplishing work objectives.

4. *Help top performers tie in their activities with those of others.* Help to coordinate working relationships for optimum effectiveness, as top performers always want to work at full effectiveness. They need full support from other organizational departments and units, and often the manager has to see that they get it in the most efficient manner.

5. *Provide top producers with all the support and required resources they need to be effective.* Let them know that help is there if they need it. Employees will reach out further when they know they can get help if they find themselves overextended. When they aren't sure that help will be available, they tend to hold back, and never operate at peak potential. They attempt the more difficult and challenging problems when they know that their efforts will be reinforced when required. This helps to boost their productivity significantly.

6. *Help top performers in their self-development.* It is best, when you work with these employees, to help them develop capabilities that will be important on advanced assignments. You can help

them to identify capabilities that will be called for in the future, and offer opportunities for these capabilities to be developed.

These six steps will help you to get your top performers to do a better job and prepare for greater responsibilities. This will lead to a more efficient accomplishment of work objectives.

Working with mid-range men. Understanding how to work with and through mid-range men to accomplish work objectives is particularly important. Almost in every organization, the majority of the men fall into the mid-performance range. Even minor improvements in the mid-range group are significant in their overall impact on organizational effectiveness, as a result of the multiplier effect involved. The first step is to determine which direction each employee is moving—either up or down. The second step is to determine each individuals career commitment—whether there are any clear cut goals. If they are to improve, they must want to do a better job and plan for the future. The third step is to make a list of each individual's strengths and drawbacks. Armed with all this information, you must determine whether, within the scope of his interests and capabilities, the employee is positioned to carry his share of the workload and to improve his level of performance as the days go by. Proper placement is a critical element for the mid-range performer. Improper placement makes employees mid-range or poor level performers because their positions are not aligned with their capabilities and interests.

Mid-range performers who aren't properly placed should be transferred to positions appropriate to their interests and capabilities; otherwise, they will continue to adversely affect organizational performance. Those who are properly placed should be teamed up with top performers. You can work through your top performers when helping mid-range performers do a better job. This helps to further develop top performers by giving them a change. They will learn how to help others, which will multiply their effectiveness. Employee development is a chain reaction. It can't occur in isolation. Opportunities for the most capable men to develop experience in working through others helps to develop the entire work group. Such an approach will also help to give you more time for result oriented activities by reducing the time to be spent by you in improving and developing mid-range performers.

Many mid-range performers have good potential, but may fall on the wayside because they can't get the attention they need. Continuing counsel from top performers under your guidance would help such men to build their capabilities and performance.

WORKING WITH POOR PERFORMERS

Poor performers are management mistakes. Either they should not have been hired for the job, or they have been placed on the wrong job. Either way, poor performers are products of poor placement.

Some mid-range performers turn into poor performers if their development is neglected. Had they been developed to tackle their job effectively or transferred to an assignment more in line with their interest and capabilities, they would not have become poor performers.

In dealing with poor performers, we have four options: (1) to rehabilitate, (2) to restructure assignments, (3) to relocate, or (4) to release. The action taken would depend upon the strengths and weaknesses of the employee and the particular situation. As a manager, you can't afford to spend too much time working with poor performers. Rapid and efficient handling of this problem is in the best interest of the organization and all concerned, including the poor performers. [4]

Managers who make good use of their time to successfully accomplish work objectives know whom to work with and how to work with them. By now it would be apparent that a manager's major emphasis should be through his top performers. Work accomplishment is greatest when you work with your top performers. It is with them that a 10 percent improvement in performance means the most. These employees can help others in the work group, and need to learn how to do so as a part of their own self-development.

Although working with top performers is the most satisfying, the individuals who need the most help are the mid-range employees. And since they are in the majority in almost every organization, this assumes added significance. Even small improvements are rewarding in their overall impact on organizational effectiveness because of the large multiplier effect involved.

---

[4] Please see Chapter 12, "How to Manage 'Problem' People," for a detailed discussion on how to deal with poor performers.

Poor producers are a special case—the management misplacements. You must put poor performers in a situation that will help optimize work accomplishment. While the best solution at times may seem to release them, this is often not the solution. Good employees may be performing poorly simply because they are not matched with their present assignment. Restructuring assignments or relocation to another job sometimes helps to utilize an intrinsically good employee and turn him into a top performer.

By following the approach outlined above, you will be able to work better with and through your people to effectively accomplish organizational work objectives.

Chapter 9

HOW TO GET THE MOST FROM NATURAL COMPETITION

Today's business environment is becoming extremely competitive. This has its impact on the organizational work group in making its members compete with each other to exploit opportunities both within and outside their organization. An understanding of the natural competitive and cooperative instincts exhibited by individuals in work groups can be extremely beneficial. This can help you to plan for competitive reactions in your work group and use them positively to motivate employees and get better performance.

THE RELATIONSHIP BETWEEN COMPETITION & COOPERATION

Why do people compete or cooperate? Before we can hope to understand why an individual will sometimes strive against, and at other times, strive with others, we must review why he strives at all.

Just why an individual will strive to attain one goal and not another has always been somewhat of a mystery. This mystery has been lessened to a great extent by the motivational studies done by people like Maslow, McClelland, McGregor, etc. Their research and theories have helped managers understand what motivates and demotivates employees in an organizational environment.[1] For our purpose of understanding competitive and cooperative behavior, we

---

[1] Please see Chapter 2, "How to Deal with What Other People Want," for a detailed discussion on employee motivation.

need only to realize that every individual has discrepancies or gaps between his levels of achievement and his levels of aspiration. Motivation is a function of what the individual now is or has and what he would like to be or have.

The level of achievement or attainment is the sum total of the individual's present attainments, not as viewed by others, but as viewed by himself. This is what really matters in his motivational drive. Thus a subordinate may actually consider his job extremely important, much more than it really may be. He is less likely to be motivated to develop himself toward greater levels of authority and responsibility than one who looks at his job realistically, provided both have the same levels of aspiration. The level of aspiration represents a person's urge or drive to achieve certain goals or ends as he himself sees them. For example, the desire to have more money, recognition and esteem than one possesses at any time is a level of aspiration common to most employees. Levels of aspiration appear in various forms in different employees and at different stages in their development. In the average employee, there is a tremendous urge to raise the level of achievement to that of aspiration, and then in turn to have a still higher aspiration.

When an individual competes or cooperates with others, he does it in order to close the gap between his level of aspiration and attainment by achieving certain goals. He will neither compete nor cooperate unless the situation seems to affect the discrepancy between his two levels.

In some cultural environments, individuals seem to compete for the sake of competing and apparently not to gain either material or social rewards. Competition in this fashion is self-sustaining. The competitive activity is pursuing goals becomes a continuous need to prove oneself superior to others. This stems from the will to conquer, the impulse to fight, or the desire to succeed for the sake of success itself. When such a competitive drive exists in an employee, his approach to work will always be competitive. If this drive is supported by rational behavior, it can prove beneficial to the work group; otherwise it may result in undesirable and dysfunctional behavior.

It has been established that in an individual the will to cooperate or compete stems from the motivation to close the gap between the levels of aspiration and those of attainment. This is true of all competitive and cooperative situations. Let us now see what makes an individual attempting to close the gap between his levels of achievement and aspiration decide to compete or cooperate.

UNDERSTANDING WHY YOUR PEOPLE COMPETE OR COOPERATE

Your people will compete in a given situation when they are aware that the goals sought cannot be shared or they are unwilling to share them. Conversely, they will cooperate if they are aware that the goals sought can be shared and will be best attained by working with each other. The goals may be material ones such as a group bonus, individual prizes, pay raise, monetary rewards, etc. Or the goals may be to get recognition, prestige, an award, appreciation, etc. Oftentimes, goals contain elements of both.

To give a simple example, your people will compete in a situation where you specify that the best individual performance will be given an award. In the same situation, they will cooperate if you specify that on attainment of the group objective, each individual will receive a share in the group reward. These rewards need not be monetary. In fact, opportunities for recognition often motivate far more than monetary incentives could.

Let us now enumerate the different circumstances under which you can expect your people to cooperate or compete.

In a work group, employees will cooperate with one another when:

1. They are striving to achieve the goals that can be shared.
2. They are *required* to achieve the goal in nearly equal amounts by management.
3. They can perform better when the goal can be achieved in equal amounts and
4. They are socially and psychologically very close to each other.

Your people will compete with one another when:

1. They are striving to achieve the same goal that is scarce.
2. They are prevented by management from achieving this goal in equal amounts.
3 They perform better when the goal can be achieved in unequal amounts and
4. They are socially and psychologically distant from each other.

This understanding of under what conditions individuals in a group cooperate or compete can help you to promote the desired kind of behavior for different situations to help achieve work objectives efficiently.

George R., the national sales manager of a large marketing organization, wanted to develop both competitive and cooperative efforts in the different sales teams across the country. To do this, he instituted an individual award of a fancy portable tape recorder for the top three producers in each team who exceeded their sales budgets. In addition, George promised an award for each individual in those teams that exceeded their quarterly sales budgets. This was a tremendous success, as the desirable aspects of both competition and cooperation were introduced to motivate superior performance. Each individual team and its members aspired for recognition and the awards which went with it. They attempted to raise their attainment levels to achieve this end, which gave national sales a tremendous boost. Individual competition was promoted by introducing a scarce goal—a limited number of tape recorders per team. Cooperative effort was at the same time encouraged by introducing a group goal which could be shared individually. This helped to increase sales by over 30% on a national basis.

By understanding the different conditions under which people cooperate or compete, you can establish the goals, rules of the situation and the performance requirements to create a competitive, cooperative or desirable mix of both types of behavior in your work group.

HOW TO COUNTER PERSONAL COMPETITION

Personal competition can best be countered by anticipating it. Anticipating it correctly and in time will help you to combat it successfully. The relevant questions which arise in a situation of personal competition are

1. In what manner can you expect your competitors to behave?
2. What considerations or factors will affect the quality and quantity of competion you are likely to receive from different individuals?

An understanding of the answers to these questions is necessary before you can correctly anticipate and successfully counter personal competition.

You can expect personal competition from those competitive individuals who seek the same scarce goals as you do. Thus, you are likely to get personal competition from your peers for promotion to the next higher management slot because it is a scarce goal. That one position has a number of aspirants. In fact, you can expect competition from individuals at all levels and in different areas—whenever the criteria of scarce goals is met.

Other examples of competitive areas may be organizational recognition, performance comparisons, awards for excellence, being closest to the top boss, etc. An individual will compete when he wants to achieve a goal which cannot be shared equally, and when his attitude and skill spur him on to competition rather than acceptance.

You have to see in your own situation the form in which individual competition is present or is likely to arise. This will help you to pinpoint clearly existing and potential individual competitors who also desire to attain your goals.

Your individual competitors will behave according to what they perceive are the rules of the situation. Their behavior will be dependent partly on accepted organizational rules of "fair competition," and partly on their own value systems. Thus, social and cultural values of an individual as well as his past, culturally conditioned experience will determine the way he competes with you.

The other considerations or factors which will affect the quantity and quality of competition you receive from an individual are listed below.

1. *Discrepancy between achievements and aspiration.* The greater the commitment and discrepancy between the goal being actively sought by your competitor and his present attainment level, the fiercer the competition you may expect. The attitude of the competitor toward his own level of aspiration, i.e., the importance to him of achieving it, is an important factor in determining how he will compete with you.

2. *Knowledge.* The attitude toward the level of aspiration is affected by the individual's knowledge concerning the goal which that level represents. The greater this knowledge, the more quality and expertise will be reflected in his competitive behavior.

3. *Attitude.* Competitive behavior will be affected by the attitude of the individual towards others. Thus, the hated competitor may be pushed aside with great bitterness, which would not be shown to a neutral or friendly competitor. This means that the form of competition depends a great deal on who is competing for the same goal. The form of competition, the insinuation, the struggle or entreaty used in reaching the goal will be affected by the individual's attitude toward the competitor. Sometimes this attitude may cause an alteration in the expected competitive response and even in the goals to be sought. Thus, an individual may decide not to compete with one of his peers who is a friend, and he may change his own goals so that they do not conflict with those of his friend.

4. *Skill.* The quantity and quality of competition from an individual will be partially dependent on his "skill" in the particular situation. The concept of "skill" here is a broad one. It refers not only to the mechanical or technical ability to perform a given task, but also to certain techniques or knacks of competing practiced by the individual to suit different competitive situations.

It is interesting to note that an individual competes only when he feels that he has a reasonable chance of success with someone of approximately equal skill.

Thus, your opponent's discrepancy or motivation to achieve the goals you are seeking, his knowledge, attitudes and skill, as well as the rules of the situation and his value system will determine how he competes with you.

To counter personal competition, the steps would be as follows:

1. First make out a list of existing or potential competitors in different areas of your activity based on the criteria discussed. These will be individuals seeking the same scarce goals as you are, and having the skill and attitude to compete with you.

2. Anticipate each individual competitor's behavior based on the factors analyzed above (i.e., on the discrepancy, knowledge, attitude and skill of each competitor).

3. Plan and implement a strategy to strengthen your position and combat anticipated competitive behavior.

4. Take the initiative and act without delay to achieve the scarce goals.

5. Review competitive behavior and revise strategy in light of the progress made in Step 4.

6. Repeat this cycle of steps periodically on a quarterly,

semiannual or annual basis depending upon the organizational situation and your goals.

Combating personal competition in a systematic manner can often be the key to achieving your desired goals. The above 6-step approach provides you with a method to systematically and effectively combat personal competition, and thereby assists you in successfully achieving your goals.

PLANNING FOR COMPETITIVE REACTIONS IN YOUR GROUP

We have already discussed under what situations people in a group will compete or cooperate. Broadly speaking, people will cooperate when they are given an opportunity to share in the achievement of goals. They will tend to compete when they seek the same goal which cannot be shared. We have seen how one national sales manager used his understanding of competitive and cooperative behavior to generate a desirable mix of both competition and cooperation in his sales organization.

While planning for competitive reactions in your group, it is also important to consider both individual attitudes as well as group size.

Individual attitudes in your group are important as they will govern the way the total group behaves. These attitudes are deeply rooted in each personality and are a sum total of an individual's reactions to his life experience. If cooperative ties have been allowed to develop, and the individual value system places cooperation as being more desirable than competition, then competitive reactions to the introduction of scarce goals will be less than desirable. This means that you cannot hope to get superior performance from a work group where cooperative ties are very strong by introducing competitive individual awards. In such cases, both group goals, as well as individual goals, need to be introduced to get the most from natural competition without destroying cooperative ties, as was illustrated in the case of the successful national sales manager. Alternately, you may need to motivate performance more through inter-group competition than through individual competition.

Let us see how one manager did this to get a competitive reaction in his close knit group.

The sales manager in charge of government sales at a branch sales office of a large organization wanted to push the sale of a new and exciting product which had been selling poorly. He considered introducing an award for the most successful individual in his team in promoting sales of the new product during the coming month. He wondered, however, if that would have any significant motivational impact, as his work group members were a close knit group with great regard for each other's professionalism. He knew that in the past, efforts to spur healthy individual competition achieved only moderate to poor results. He decided to use the cooperative spirit of the group to generate a strong competitive reaction. By getting together with the sales manager of the commercial sales team, he worked out a competition between the two teams. The team getting the most unit orders for the new product per man would win the contest. The winning team would be hosted to dinner by the general manager, with the losing team paying for the drinks. The professional pride of both teams was aroused. Individuals in both teams worked closely together to boost the sales of the new product. Weekly meetings were held by each of the sales managers to review the competitive position of both teams. This helped to further generate a motivation to win in each team. In that one month, the branch sales office sold more units of the new product than it had in the past nine months. Sales budgets were exceeded by both teams. The sales manager of government sales achieved his objective of arousing a competitive reaction in his group to boost sales of the new product. He did this through inter-group competition rather than individual competition, because he had correctly assessed the strong individual attitude of cooperation within the group.

The size of the group also has an impact on its competitive or cooperative behavior. As the group grows larger, the common denominator of interest becomes less specific, and agitation for sub-groups, formal or informal, soon appears. Increased membership of a group means that it will be easier to get competitive reactions. This is because in a large group it is less likely that individuals will have the same goals or be able to retain affiliate contact with one another. Thus, it is easier to get individual competitive reactions in a large group than in a small one. What this implies is that the size of your group will determine the approach you can best use to generate competitive reactions to get the most from natural competition. If your work group is small and close knit, you can motivate desirable competitive reactions by introducing both individual and group goals, only group goals, or inter-group competition, depending upon the situation. If you have a large work group without strong personal ties amongst all its members, you can motivate desirable competitive reactions by emphasizing both individual and group goals or only individual goals, depending upon the situation. In other words, shared goals for small work groups are the *predominant* motivators for getting immediate performance improvements. Successful managers, however, use both individual and group goals to get a desirable mix of both cooperative and competitive reactions in their group. Obviously, dominance of individual over group goals will be determined by the situation, the objective to be achieved, and the work group size.

By this understanding of how you can generate competitive or cooperative reactions in your work group, you can plan to achieve your work objectives with the desired motivational support of your work group.

ENCOURAGING INNOVATIVENESS THROUGH COMPETITION

Every work group has a capability to generate new ideas. However, very often there is no avenue to express new ideas or introduce innovativeness. Innovativeness can best be encouraged in a work group by:

(1) having a scheme or method to record new ideas, discuss them, improve on them and finally to implement them.
(2) rewarding innovativeness through recognition and material benefits.

Generally, a competitive arrangement to judge the best innovations or ideas serves both purposes very well.

Let us see how a very successful manager used a simple competitive tool to encourage innovativeness wherever he went.

Art B. had developed a reputation for being immensely successful in handling new ideas wherever he went. As a manager with a large multinational corporation, he had had occasion for many a varied assignment. In each assignment, he had shown excellent improvements in performance. He attributed his success to working well with people and being able to benefit from their expertise and strengths to bring about improvements and desirable innovations. He used a very simple tool effectively to encourage innovation and improve performance. Wherever he went, he introduced an idea recognition scheme. All ideas submitted were reviewed by Art and discussed in work group meetings with all concerned. Those that were found promising were implemented, with full participation of the employees concerned. At the end of every quarter, all ideas implemented were reviewed, and the most useful innovation was awarded a cash prize. In addition, really outstanding ideas, if any, were given special cash awards, depending upon their significance. An idea recognition committee, with three elected members from amongst his people and chaired by Art, kept a log of all ideas suggested, discussed, improved upon and implemented. This committee was the one that selected the best innovation every quarter. All ideas implemented, with details of the employee concerned, were sent to the organization's news letter for publication. The award winning idea got a special write up every quarter. The idea recognition scheme provided a good vehicle for individual employees to suggest and follow up on productive ideas. The single quarterly cash award and possibility of special cash awards made employees present ideas in a polished manner. They competed very strongly and optimum benefits were the result.

All managers can encourage innovative activity amongst their people by using a competitive idea recognition approach such as the one just illustrated. The rewards offered for outstanding ideas may be monetary, but do not always have to be. Recognition is quite a motivator and, if used properly, can reduce or even eliminate the need for cash or material awards. Generally speaking, however, wherever feasible, cash awards should be offered in addition to a worthwhile recognition opportunity, as money and recognition together stimulate very strong motivation.

Individual and group competition in any form tend to generate new approaches to doing things better. Therefore, even in a general sense, competitive activity breeds innovation. This tendency to innovate needs to be encouraged by: (1) listening to new ideas which are prompted by strong competition drives and (2) providing support to make desirable innovative approaches possible.

Competitive behavior coupled with a rational and positive attitude often helps to bring out innovative ideas in organizational groups. Let us review an instance where this was vividly demonstrated:

In the example cited earlier, where the sales manager of government sales used inter-group competition to help boost the sales of the new product, an interesting additional benefit accrued from the competition. During the competitive drive between the two sales teams, the commercial group developed a demonstration kit for all prospects regarding the new product. This kit was very creative, as it vividly portrayed the applications of the new product in the area. The innovative idea was encouraged by the commercial team's sales manager, and the demo kits were sanctioned. Their use proved extremely beneficial. After the contest was over, they were used by both teams very effectively. The competitive reaction had helped to develop this innovative idea to get orders quickly for the new product. This innovativeness through competition was supported in the proper manner by the manager concerned, and hence proved to be of great value in achieving increased sales of the new product.

Encouraging innovativeness through competition is, therefore, a worthwhile tool in the hands of the manager to get the most from natural competitive drives in his work group.

USING COMPETITION POSITIVELY

We have seen how competitive and cooperative behavior can be induced in a work group. Depending upon the goals to be achieved, the attitude of the persons involved and the organizational situation, you can use both individual and group competition in a positive manner.

Individual competition in a group can be created by establishing a goal to be achieved which cannot be shared, such as an individual top performance award. Group cooperation can be maintained by making sure that there are some group goals which can be shared, such as a group incentive, group recognition, group responsibility, etc. It is generally beneficial to use both individual and group goals to get a desirable mix of both competitive and cooperative behavior.

Competition, both individual and group, helps to develop individuals in as much as they extend themselves to show off their best. Furthermore, competitive situations help to foster new ideas which, when recognized and supported, can result in extremely beneficial innovations.

Thus, you can use competition positively by balancing it with cooperative behavior to achieve overall organizational objectives, to motivate your people to give off their best, and to promote innovativeness.

By understanding the organizational subculture and the individuals in your work group, you can introduce suitable competitive reactions, as illustrated and discussed, to get the most from natural competition.

To use competition positively, you need to take the following four steps:

Step 1. Review the overall objectives you want to achieve in relation to existing organizational rules, persons and performance levels.

Step 2. Determine your work group attitude through reviewing each individual's achievement discrepancy, knowledge, attitude and skill levels.

Step 3. With the above as a base, determine the mix of individual and group goals you should use to get the desired competitive and cooperative behavior in your group. Plan also to encourage and support individual self-development in the competitive environment. Also plan to encourage and utilize innovative ideas arising through competition by using an idea recognition approach and providing your own support.

Step 4. Review the results achieved from the introduction of individual and group goals to achieve overall objectives. Adapt goals to changed organizational needs, rules, persons and performance levels as and when necessary.

The above four-step approach, when adapted to your situation, will help you to get the most from natural competition in your organizational environment.

Chapter 10

HOW TO MINIMIZE PEOPLE'S RESISTANCE TO CHANGE

- The seating arrangements in an office need to be rearranged to accommodate three new clerks.
- As a result of the studies made by the industrial engineering department, the operator of a paper coating machine is required to operate two new coating machines simultaneously, instead of operating one old paper coating machine, as had been the custom.
- A sales manager is told by the sales director that within three months he should retrain and reassign salesmen on a regionwise basis, rather than on the existing productwise basis, in view of the new marketing strategy adopted by the company.
- The purchasing manager of a plant is asked by the plant manager to introduce the changes in the inventory control system advised by a firm of management consultants.
- The general manager of a sewing machine factory announces that, as a part of the drive to improve the profitability of the factory's operations, a fresh evaluation of the production bonus scheme is to be made to set up new production and wastage standards.
- The board of directors of a company decides to diversify the organization's principal business activities by entering the field of office duplicating equipment.

These and many other similar situations are examples of the numerous changes which managers are required to deal with and implement. If you were the manager who was asked to implement some of these changes, you would find a number of similarities in each one of them. Each of these instances relates to the introduction of change, the need for which arises from the desire to achieve improvements and benefits.

All such changes invariably involve and affect people. In every case, the benefits and improvements which result are dependent on the behavior of both the managers and the people affected. Even though change is a fact of life and is often very desirable, individuals and groups have a natural tendency to resist change unless it is clearly and assuredly for the better. Changes tend to generate feelings of uncertainty and doubt among those involved. As most managerial decisions involve some change, whether it be minor or major, temporary or permanent, this resistance becomes a common problem which the manager consciously or unconsciously has to face in the organizational setting. Therefore, in dealing with and managing people successfully, it becomes important to understand how to minimize their resistance to desirable and necessary changes.

UNDERSTANDING WHY PEOPLE FEAR CHANGE

All individuals need security. Security comes from a familiar and unchanging environment. Therefore, each individual is apprehensive of change and tends to resist it to protect his known status.

The basic causes for resistance are both the *imagined* and *real* effects of the change, together with the manner in which it is being brought about. Actually the change is often only the symbol of what is being opposed. It is necessary for a manager to get a clear understanding of why people fear change before he can take effective steps to minimize their resistance to change.

An individual's apprehensions are based upon attitudes which result from seven interrelating factors:

1. *Predisposed feeling about change.*

People react differently to change. Some individuals are suspicious and distrustful. Others are self-confident and approach change with objective questions based on the realities of the situation. A manager can deal with such reactions from different people if he understands what causes their attitudes to be different.

Right from childhood all individuals face changes which they naturally tend to resist. Take a lollipop away from a child and the result would be a scream of protest. Even a promise of two lollipops an hour later will not placate him. He wants immediate gratification. The memories of unpleasant childhood experiences and of the associated feelings of resistance, suspicion and distrust tend to persist during adulthood.

All adults have gone through unpleasant childhood experiences. Nevertheless, the attitudes of each adult tend to vary widely. This is so because each individual has been handled differently by his parents and has different inherited strengths and weaknesses. A child who was forced to conform to unreasonable demands by unyielding parents will tend to regard almost every change with suspicion and fear. These feelings would tend to persist throughout his life. Such an adult would react to a change with unrelated personal fears and questions. As a manager, you would not gain very much by using logical explanations and arguments with such an individual. You can minimize his resistance only by assuring him that he would not be harmed by the change. If you can go further and show him how he will benefit from the change, you are likely to get his cooperation and support as well.

On the other hand, a child whose parents were patient, flexible and understanding, would as an adult tend to regard change in a more attractive light. He would also question change, but in an objective and realistic manner. With such persons it is only necessary to explain the need and usefulness of the change to get necessary support and acceptance.

2. *Feelings of insecurity.*

Feelings of security or insecurity result from an individual's cumulative experiences since birth, and become a part of his personality. They also reflect to a limited extent an individual's financial situation. Clearly, anyone with independent means is less likely to fear change affecting his job than the person relying solely on his wage earnings.

Such feelings have a deep impact on many aspects of an individual's behavior. They can cause a person to have fears without objective logical justification. Such a person would find more reasons for objecting to a proposed change than would someone who felt more secure. They also affect his self-confidence, resourcefulness and initiative. Finally, they determine how flexible and adaptable one is.

If a manager is able to recognize illogical and unrealistic fears, he can then take appropriate steps to generate trust and confidence in the individuals concerned regarding how the change is likely to affect them.

3. *Cultural beliefs and norms.*

All of us operate in several different societies. These are the work group, the department or division of the organization, the organization as a whole, the community, the region, the nation, etc. Each of these societies had identifiable social and cultural beliefs and behavioral norms which influence individual attitudes towards change. In any business organization, as well as in its sub-divisions, there are cultural beliefs concerned with the value of perpetuating certain practices. As in primitive societies, these beliefs are accepted implicitly, and are rarely, if ever, questioned.

Some examples of cultural beliefs and behavioral norms that exist in some business organizations are:

- Skilled craftsmen must have 'mates' or helpers to assist them.
- Long service with a single organization is basically desirable.
- Perquisites should be proportional to the status of the job.
- The length of an employee's service in an organization should determine his "rights" to tenure, benefits, and advancement.

Such cultural beliefs should not be labelled good or bad per se, but looked at in the context of the local environment and what motivates the different societies interacting with each other in the organizational setting. Treating them as being backward or irrelevant can generate tremendous resistance to management actions and changes. Whether good or bad, the prevailing cultural beliefs and behavioral norms become an important factor to be tackled by the manager, especially when they are pertinent to any change. This is illustrated by the following actual incidence.

In a particular plant, skilled workers were given helpers to assist them. A change was introduced by the plant manager whereby the skilled workers stood to appreciably increase their earnings by foregoing the need of the helpers. A few of the helpers with considerable experience were promoted to skilled workers, and others were absorbed to fill certain vacancies and strengthen other sections.

No one was retrenched. The plant manager was quite confident that his change would be welcomed, as it stood to benefit all concerned. It meant reduced expenses for the organization, higher earnings for the skilled workers, and a higher level or alternate employment to the helpers.

Nevertheless, within a few days of the introduction of the change, the skilled workers organized a protest and gave a written notice through their union of a tool down strike unless the old system was reinstated. The plant manager, by introducing the change without considering the feelings of the skilled workers, had overlooked the significance of the value which each skilled worker attached to his social status in doing only skilled work and having a helper. This value was far greater to him than the additional income which was promised as a result of the change. The skilled workers implicitly believed that they should not perform any work which is outside the boundaries of their craft. Management had to revert back to the previous system to keep the plant from closing down. They could introduce the change only after about a year, by which time they were able to change the value attached by skilled workers in having helpers. The attitude change was brought about by emphasizing the dignity attached to labor and self-help, and by citing examples of other plans and organizations where the proposed system was working well.

As a manager, therefore, you must be aware of both the existence and the potential significance of the cultural beliefs and norms prevalent in your organization and its subdivisions. With this knowledge you would be able to recognize when a specific change is in conflict with one or more of these cultural beliefs and norms. You would thus be in a better position to understand and minimize, if not avoid, such conflicts. Having recognized the possibility of a conflict you can:

1. Change the conflicting cultural belief and consequent attitudes.

2. Modify the proposed change so that it does not conflict with cultural values.

3. Adapt both the proposed change and the cultural values to suit each other as far as possible.

The specific action which you take would depend upon each particular situation.

4. *Trust in management, union and work groups.*

Another factor that influences an individual's attitudes towards change is the nature of his relationships with different individuals and subgroups in the organization. If an employee has considerable trust in his manager, he would probably have faith that whatever the change, his welfare will be looked after. On the other hand, if there is little trust, he would be fearful of a proposed change. Similarly, if he lacks confidence in his union and his workmates, he would be inwardly even more opposed to a change, as he would tend to feel that his future security depended primarily on his own ability to protect his interests.

Loyalty and trust for the company, the manager and the union are developed through a series of direct personal experiences and observations.

These are also influenced by the existing cultural beliefs. Thus, it is likely that most individuals would conform to the prevailing cultural beliefs about the insincerity and general untrustworthiness of an organization's management.

The manager must accept that if there is little trust his problems of implementing change will be difficult. He can counterbalance a "lack of trust" situation somewhat by providing explicit and firm facts and guarantees, and by a gradual introduction of change through a series of experimental trials. In situations where the manager has built up considerable trust between himself and his work group, resistance to change would tend to be far less than what might otherwise be.

5. *Historical events relevant to the change.*

An individual's attitudes toward change are also influenced by the historical events relevant to the change. Thus an organization's past policies, practices and customs, the extent to which its managements have proved themselves trustworthy, the manner in which past changes have been carried out, etc., are examples of relevant historical events in the organization which influence its people with respect to their reactions to future changes. The important historical factors of the region and nation, such as the patterns of unemployment, the extent of opportunities for alternative employment, the amount of government involvement or control with respect to business, etc., also have an impact on the attitudes of people to change. People often regard past events as precedents for what is likely to occur in the future. It's therefore advantageous for the manager to be aware of the existence of past historical events relevant to a proposed change. With such knowledge, he can counterbalance the influence of those historical events which have had a potentially negative effect on the formation of attitudes. Similarly, the manager can use advantageously those past happenings that might have a beneficial effect on attitudes towards a change.

6. *Expectations and apprehensions about a particular change.*

An organization has its own needs. A most compelling need is to survive in a state of homeostatic equilibrium with its environment.[1] Thus, the need arises for improvement in products, sales volume, public image, human relations, etc. Most changes introduced by managers are aimed at meeting these ends. Such changes can, however, bring into sharp focus conflicts between both the immediate and long-term needs of the organization and those of the people involved. On the other hand, sometimes these needs will be more in harmony than in conflict. In any case, change tends to arouse apprehensions as well as expectations among those involved. A manager must be able to cope with the conflicts and questions which a change poses for different individuals. Examples of some of the questions which individuals may ask their manager before a change are:

- How effective will I be in the new setup?
- Will the new situation mean more responsibility for me? Will I receive increased recognition?
- They are asking me to do something entirely different. Can it be done?
- In terms of the change, how will others regard me? What will be my status in the eyes of others?
- In the new situation, can my future performance be judged fairly? How will it be judged?
- What will my subordinates think of me after the change? Will they alter their regard for me?
- How will customers, vendors and those outside the company regard me after the change? Will they regard this as an increase or decrease in my status in the company?
- How will my chances for advancement be affected?
- How important does the company regard the new situation?
- How much is at stake on how good a job I do?

Many such questions will concern individual expectations.

---

[1] Chris Argyris in "Understanding Human Behavior in Organizations," *Modern Organization Theory* (ed. M. Haire), Wiley, New York, 1959, emphasizes that all organizations need to change and adapt constantly to the external environment.

Others may not be realistically based, such as those arising out of feelings of insecurity. Whatever the nature of the questions, the manager will have to face them. As long as the individuals involved think of these as genuine problems they must be dealt with by the manager. It is therefore important that the manager prepare himself to answer questions regarding individual and group expectations. Failure to do so will enhance individual fears and increase resistance to the change.

7. *The manner of change.*

The manner in which a change is introduced and implemented also influences the attitudes of those involved toward it. Whenever management institutes a change, the number of orders given to subordinates tends to increase substantially. In such circumstances, people tend to lose their feelings of autonomy and self-sufficiency. Their resentment of the change becomes heightened if the orders for the change appear to be arbitrary and unilateral. When people feel that they must alter their behavior without any apparent reason, they are likely to be more stubborn in their opposition. Furthermore, if the change is presented as being irreversible and irrevocable, individual and group suspicions and fears will inevitably increase.

Insufficient information about the reasons for the change and its implications adds to individual fears about the change. When someone's mind is filled with questions about a change which remain unanswered, he is likely to invent answers. These self answers are often based on unnecessary imaginings and fears. This will cause an individual to be even more suspicious and fearful of the change than he might otherwise be.

When an employee is not treated as an individual, but merely as a member of a group, he resents the apparent lack of concern for his individual problems. [2] This resentment is channeled into negative and resistant feelings toward the change. It has been repeatedly found that whenever a superior conveys to his subordinates a feeling of confidence in them, and an interest in their individual on-the-job and off-the-job problems, it has a major

---

[2] This is based on the personal experience of the authors, and confirmed in independent studies conducted by social scientists such as R. Likert in "A Motivational Approach to a Modified Theory of Organization and Management," *Modern Organization Theory* (ed. M. Haire), Wiley, New York, 1959.

influence in positively motivating them towards the achievement of performance goals.

Finally, the timing of a change can cause tensions and fears. When sufficient time is not allowed for adjustments, those involved in a change develop apprehensions about their ability to cope with the new requirements. On the other hand, suitable timing of the change can be used by the manager to help allay the fears of the employees concerned. Let us see how this was done by one manager.

> Dave S., the new manager of the distributing department of a large corporation, had completed a major study of its distribution operations. If certain improvements were made in the methods of operation, the company would be able to distribute its products with about 800 fewer employees. The company had been subcontracting many of its distribution operations. Dave's study showed that it would be economical to directly handle about three-fourths of the total distribution activities. The contracts with most of the sub-contracting firms were coming up for renegotiation in a few months. The manager decided to time the improvement in distribution operations to coincide with the break points in these contracts. Thus, most of the employees who would have been excess could be retained by reabsorption of the work being subcontracted.

When delaying the implementation of a desirable change, the manager must remember that it should not be for an indefinite period and must always be clearly beneficial as compared with the disadvantages of its immediate implementation. In the above example, the manager timed the controversial change with a reinforcing event in the near future to avoid the fear and active resistance which would have otherwise resulted. The time before a change is actually implemented should be used to help others understand the need for change. Let us see how this can be done.

HELPING OTHERS UNDERSTAND THE NEED FOR CHANGE

We have seen what factors influence an individual's fear of change. The manager can exert varying degrees of control over the influence of these factors. However, a manager has full control over only two factors. One of these is the extent to which conflicts between the interests of the people involved and those of the organization are rationalized. The other is the manner in which the change is introduced and implemented. Before we get into the area of introducing and implementing change, let us consider how those involved can best be made to understand the need for change.

There are two methods used in practice to help those involved to understand the need and implications of a proposed change. These are (1) discussion and understanding and (2) involvement and participation.

1. Discussion and Understanding

When the people involved in a change understand as much as possible about it and its consequences, their resistance is likely to be reduced. It is up to the manager to develop this understanding.

The manager should always make use of face to face discussions both with individuals and with groups. This is the most effective technique for ensuring that answers are being given to questions of genuine concern from the employees involved. Additionally, this is the most effective means of determining how much real understanding is being achieved. The importance of creating a real understanding through discussion with all concerned is illustrated in the following example:

> A manager was temporarily successful in "selling" a change based on a complicated mathematical formula to a foreman who really did not understand it. It backfired, however, when the foreman tried to sell it to his operating people. He could not answer a number of sharp questions that they asked him. His embarrassment about this led him to resent and resist the change, so that eventually the whole idea fell through. The manager was perplexed at the apparent change of heart in the foreman, and could not understand his dogged resistance to the change, especially since the foreman was one of the best in the plant. This was unfortunate not only in terms of human relations, but of technological progress in the plant as well.

Face to face discussion at planned intervals not only helps the manager in conveying the need for a change to those involved and in answering their questions, but also gives him feedback as to what problems are likely to be faced in implementing the change.

To create the desired understanding of the change, the manager can additionally communicate the details of the change in writing through notices, circulars, posters, articles, etc., or orally through announcements, formal orientation, etc. The more complex the change, the greater should be the variety of media employed.

2. Involvement and Participation

Experience shows that when the people to be affected by a change are involved in its planning and implementation, they tend to understand and accept the need for change much better. [3] We have seen how face-to-face discussions can help to develop an understanding of change and its probable consequences. The process of participation is a method of managing based on both face-to-face discussions and involvement.

The concept of using "participation" to generate understanding and acceptance among employees has become rather fashionable in management circles, but is quite loosely understood. The objective of a participative approach is to achieve acceptance by a group of people that they are taking part in planning, initiating, and implementing a change, instead of being merely the recipients of its effects. In practice, however, participation has come to mean different things to different managers. To some, it is a device for "masterminding" people to share the viewpoint held by the manager. To other managers, it is a ritual to be observed so that there is an illusion created that the employees have some voice in what is going on and in what is happening to them. Such views are quite different from the true meaning of participation. Participation must truly and basically be a means for the manager to exercise his responsibility to the people who work under him and with him, in order to provide them with a sense of belonging based on human dignity. True participation cannot be created by management instruction. Real participation depends upon the feelings and attitudes of the people concerned. The art of assembling a group of people for discussion does not mean that participation has been generated or is being motivated. Furthermore, it is not correct to assume that under all circumstances employees would want to participate. Studies of some business organizations have shown that in certain work groups, the need to be involved in the planning and implementation of desirable changes is absent or subordinated to other more pressing needs, such as job security. [4]

---

[3] This is based on the experience of the authors, as well as of numerous other managers and behavioral scientists. See for example, G. Strauss and L. Sayles, *Personnel, The Human Problems of Management*, Prentice-Hall, Englewood Cliffs, New Jersey, 1960, p. 150.

[4] C. Argyris had vividly demonstrated this in a study of employee behavior reported in *Modern Organization Theory*, Wiley, New York, 1959, p. 149.

When and how, then, can a manager ensure and use true participation? The following are the basic prerequisite conditions which must all be met for true participation to take place:

I. The employees involved must want to participate.
II. The manager must feel secure in his position so as to invite suggestions and participation from his subordinates.
III. The manager must not have a commitment to any one course of action. He must be open-minded to possible alternative approaches for bringing about the desired change.
IV. The manager must be willing to give credit and recognition openly to all who make contributions of merit in regard to the change.
V. The employees must be willing to voice their comments and to offer suggestions. Mere acceptance will not work with people who are passive and apathetic.

If all these conditions are not present, the manager would do well to be cautious in the use of participation as a management technique for generating understanding and acceptance of coming changes. He would profit in such situations by using face-to-face discussions to answer questions and clarify the need for change. Wherever feasible, he should use individual or group consultation to generate a fuller understanding of the problem that a change is expected to solve. Employee consultation is based on the very correct, practical consideration that the man actually doing a job on a day to day basis is usually more knowledgeable about it than anyone else. Let us see how employee consultation has worked in practice.

The manager of an auto accessories plant was facing an unusually stubborn problem. Product quality had fallen off, and none of the engineering staff was able to find a solution. Expensive consultants also failed to stop the increased flow of rejects. The manager had become conscious of his tendency to run the plant without employee consultation or participation. He decided to change his tactics to crack this tough problem, and asked for ideas and suggestions from his employees in a plant wide meeting. After a painful silence, during which the "yes" men were looking around for someone to speak up, two individuals, generally viewed as incompetent, quietly but definitely took the problem apart, brought out the true causes, and laid out the solution. The manager listened to them with amazement and appreciation. He had not even known the capabilities of these men before he decided to change his approach and get them involved in the running of the plant through the process of consultation.

In the process of consultation, the manager may accept or reject suggestions on their merit and worth. However, if an employee's suggestion is rejected, he must be made to understand why. Then consultation can still be very productive, even if the employees' suggestions need to be rejected. There are three reasons for this. First, the fact that an employee has an opportunity to express himself and be given serious attention is very beneficial to his attitude and morale. Also, by understanding why his suggestion is not acceptable, the employee can reach a better understanding of the change. Finally, he may be encouraged to offer better suggestions for the future.

If participation is to operate at a deeper level (where all the prerequisite conditions exist), it should include some involvement of the concerned employees in diagnosing the particular problems underlying the need for a change. The benefits of doing this are illustrated in the following case:

> The manager of a plant manufacturing a wide variety of consumer products felt that the workers had developed negative attitudes about their jobs due to poor supervisory practices. He called a meeting of the supervisors to tackle this problem, and set up a method incorporating their suggestions for diagnosing the causes of these negative attitudes and low morale. Each supervisor then returned to his section, and gathered facts for diagnosing the causes of the negative attitudes among his workers. Later, the supervisors were called to a meeting to report their findings. At the meeting, their enthusiasm for change in their own practices was high because they had participated in gathering the facts relevant to their problems. They did not hesitate to bring in changes and improvements in their own practices and objectives in order to remove the negative attitudes of their workers, because they had participated in diagnosing their own problem.

People will generally act constructively on the basis of information gathered by themselves, rather than on the basis of information gathered by others and conveyed to them.

As a manager, you can effectively use face-to-face discussions, written and oral communications, employee involvement and participation in many different ways to help others understand the need for change.

HOW TO DISCUSS COMING CHANGES IN GROUPS

In the process of managing people, a manager often needs to discuss coming changes with groups. If he can do this well, the successful implementation of these changes is faciliated. This, in turn, undoubtedly contributes to his overall success as a manager.

There are five essential steps which, as a manager, you must take to successfully discuss coming changes in groups.

1. *Understanding the change yourself.*

Before a manager can discuss a change, he must first fully understand what is about to happen. He must be able to answer the following questions:

- What is to be done and why?
- What are the different ways in which it can be accomplished?
- What will be changed as a consequence?

If he doesn't know some of the answers, then he must get them from his boss and others concerned. After getting the answers to these questions, he will be able to distinguish the means from the ends.

In most situations, it is the ends or objectives that are important. Both immediate and long range objectives must be noted. Provided that the means used are ethical and moral, it matters little which are employed. What does matter is how well the desired long range objectives can be accomplished by the different means under consideration.

A manager must remain as flexible as possible in selecting or modifying the means for achieving the desired objectives. He can do this if he maintains a clear separation in his mind between the objectives and the methods for their accomplishment. When such a distinction is blurred, the methods can themselves become the primary objectives. When this occurs, the manager can become so committed to a particular method that he loses both flexibility and objectivity, which are essential to the success of a change. To remain flexible and objective, the manager must not only separate the methods from the objectives, but must also remain open to incorporating worthwhile suggestions from the groups in which the change is to be discussed.

This raises the question of how discussion groups should be formed.

2. *Forming discussion groups.*

The formation of discussion groups depends upon the particular organizational setup and the nature of a proposed change. Every manager needs to form a group or groups from amongst his immediate subordinates to discuss a coming change. If you have a number of sections or departments reporting to you, then these discussion groups would naturally tend to be along the lines of sectional, departmental, and organization committees, depending upon your position in the organizational hierarchy. These committees could also serve as discussion groups for other similar changes. Generally, these committees or groups would also be responsible for implementing the change. How this is done will be a matter to be discussed.

In case the nature of the change is such that it affects other departments, then representatives of those departments should be invited to participate in the discussion group or groups.

Having decided on the group or groups in which a coming change is to be discussed, the manager should call for a preliminary meeting in which all concerned individuals should be present. Depending upon whether the requirement for change is a sudden development or not, the manager should give sufficient background information to all group members. If this can be done, then the employees concerned would be better able to offer useful suggestions during the course of the discussion.

3. *Planning for the discussion.*

The manager must plan in advance what is to be discussed. For this he must do the following:

1. Prepare to explain the coming change in terms of what matters to the employees concerned. He should equip himself to explain the answers to the various questions he posed initially in order to fully understand the change himself.

2. Anticipate possible questions and objections, as well as the extent of resistance likely to be offered by different

individuals. He can thereby prepare to answer expected objections, and minimize anticipated resistance by clearing doubts and fears, giving required assurances, etc.

3. Consider the method or possible methods of implementing the change, and plan on improving these based on any useful suggestions and comments made by his employees during the discussions.

4. Decide how best he can point out the advantages and added incentives, if any, which the change would bring to the employees, when it is successfully implemented.

Having prepared himself for the discussion, the manager can then plan how he is going to conduct it.

4. *Conducting the discussion.*

It is best to have the initial discussion in a large group comprising all employees concerned with the change. Thereafter, if need be, the discussion can be continued in smaller groups formed on a sectional, departmental or interdepartmental basis, depending upon the nature of the change.

During the discussion, the manager should provide the necessary background about the reason and objectives of the change, and how it is likely to affect those present. The manager can then discuss group incentives, if any, and the expected participation of his employees in making and reviewing suggestions for improving the effectiveness of the change. The discussion of group incentives becomes really important for major changes. Research in the running of business operations has proven that group incentives, as well as employee participation in planning and implementing all signficiant changes, contribute greatly to dramatically increasing the overall efficiency of an organization. A little later, an instance of where this was actually done in one organization will be discussed.

The manager should then go into the possible method or methods of implementing the change, and invite questions and suggestions from the employees. In case the change is one which would need to be implemented over a considerable period of time, he should also discuss, where suitable conditions exist, the means of continuing employee participation for improving the effectiveness of the change. This is often done by the formation of standing committees. These meet periodically to discuss suggestions submitted by individual employees, and to overcome problems and obstacles to the efficient implementation of the change. The manager should form the standing committees, if necessary, and allocate responsibilities for any follow-up that needs to be done arising from the discussion. Throughout the discussion, the manager must allow ample opportunities for getting employee reactions, questions and suggestions.

Let us now see, by an actual example, how discussing coming changes in groups can bring amazingly good results.

> The manager of a printing plant had tried to introduce a conveyor system. The design engineers had developed the plans without consulting any of the employees. From the very start, the system failed to work properly, and there was no interest from the employees in making it work.
>
> To invoke the interest of the employees, the manager decided to discuss the conveyor system afresh with them in a group. He had a small scale model of the proposed system layout made to provide the necessary background information for the employees at the time of the discussion. At the discussion meeting, after he had given the necessary details of what was expected from the new system and why, he encouraged those present to suggest improvements and speak their mind on the proposed change. Based on these comments which came forth, a joint production committee was formed which made modifications to eliminate problems the engineers had overlooked. The engineers were happy with the interest and cooperation the new system had aroused, and installed the new system incorporating the useful suggestions they had received. Needless to say, the new system ran successfully, and improved the plant productivity and the earnings of the employees appreciably.

The manager in the preceding example admitted that he had actually got the idea to discuss the new system with the employees concerned in a management development seminar, where he learned about the Scanlon plan. The Scanlon plan is named after the man who devised it, and is primarily a program with two basic elements:

I. Participation of employees through group discussions, joint committees, etc., to improve the effectiveness of the operation or change, and

II. Some form of group incentive.

It is an approach to managing people that gears both the attitude and capability of all employees toward carrying out changes for improvements. The manager, in fact, can use this approach to improve his overall operating effectiveness. There is no standard approach to the "group" incentive. Typically, it is a wage formula that provides for every employee (sometimes including managers) to receive a monthly bonus based on monthly improvements in operating effectiveness. This is generally measured in terms of output to total payroll costs, and is developed through discussions and negotiations with the employees concerned or their union representatives. Once in operation, it also provides a feedback to the employees as to how well they are achieving their common desired objectives.

The great strength of an approach of this type rests on the participation of employees, which is achieved primarily through discussions in groups and committees formed at various levels in the organization. Suggestions affecting the organization as a whole are sent up to the organizational level committee, comprised of members of the top management and employee leadership. Notable suggestions are rewarded at each level. Suggestions are rejected only after careful consideration, and are accompanied by full explanations. This overall approach can work only if the manager can abandon traditional prerogatives and attitudes, and if, as discussed earlier, favorable conditions exist for participation. The experience of managers who have used this approach has shown that this has made possible the introduction of changes which the manager could not have introduced in the pre Scanlon approach days. [5] Wherever used, this approach minimizes resistance to change because it involves people in the process of creating change, rather than imposing it on them.

A SYSTEMATIC APPROACH TO MAKING CHANGES

Obviously, there can be no standard method for making changes, as no single approach can take into account the enormous variability of the factors present in every situation and organization. Secondly, there are different personal styles of managing, and this factor precludes the possibility of any single method. Nevertheless, it is possible that a manager can be helped to develop a systematic approach to the way he implements changes.

---

[5] Douglas McGregor has corroborated this in F.G. Lesieur (ed.), *The Scanlon Plan: A Frontier in Labor-Management Cooperation*, Wiley, New York, 1958, pp. 89-94.

There are certain essential considerations which a manager must take into account for successfully implementing a change, irrespective of the situation or organization in which he is in. These considerations can be looked upon as a personal checklist which a manager must use to ensure that he has overlooked nothing of importance either in his planning or implementation of a desirable change.

Basically, a manager has to take the following five steps for successfully realizing any change:

I Analyzing and planning the change
II Communicating the change
III Gaining acceptance
IV Making the initial transition
V Consolidating and following up

Analyzing and planning the change

The first step a manager should take for introducing or implementing any significant change is to develop a clear understanding of the change: its basis, objectives, scope and implications. We have already discussed how he can go about doing this.

Having understood the basis and nature of the proposed change, the manager can proceed to estimate its effects on those involved and their probable reactions. Based on his estimates of the difficulties and resistance to be encountered, he can plan a program for minimizing them through helping others understand the need for change and discussing the change in groups. This procedure, discussed earlier, requires the manager to regard the change from the viewpoint of those likely to be affected by the change. The manager must plan to eliminate many of the objectionable aspects of the change and, as far as practicable, provide rewards to offset objectionable aspects which cannot be eliminated.

Finally, to complete the stage of analyzing and planning the change, the manager must develop a tentative but specific time plan for the introduction, implementation and follow up of the desired change. This can best be done by first identifying and listing each distinct task for implementing the change. The dependent tasks must be separated from the independent ones.

Thus, the manager will find that some tasks must be completed before others are begun, and some can be carried out at any time. These should be arranged in their proper sequential and parallel relationships, and the time needed to complete each task should then be estimated. The highest priority should be given to completing those dependent tasks, which on further analysis, are critical to the achievement of the overall change. A delay in any of these "critical" elements would cause a delay in the overall change. For simple changes, the manager can put down this plan in a simple, schematic form on a sheet of paper, which serves as his master plan of action and a means of controlling and comparing actual versus planned performance. For complex changes requiring many separate tasks or steps, the manager may use the techniques of network analysis (CPM or PERT) to develop a timed plan with assigned priorities to different tasks.[6] This can either be done by the manager himself or, as is more generally the case, with the assistance of the project or staff department concerned.

The manager should involve his subordinates and key members of any relevant staff service groups in constructing a timed plan for action, and in planning a program for minimizing resistance. This involvement of the concerned and key personnel will ensure that the plan developed is realistic, and will help in its implementation by becoming the commitment of not only the manager but also of all those who participated in the planning process.

Communicating the change

The next step for the manager is to help those concerned understand the need for change through varied communication media. As discussed, these would include face-to-face discussions, employee involvement and participation, written communications, etc. At this stage, the manager would also have to deal with the union whenever pertinent.

From the manager's standpoint, the purpose of this communication should be twofold. Firstly, he must ensure that all those involved get an understanding of the reasons for the change, its

---

[6] For the technical details of the "critical path method" and "Program Evaluation and Review Technique," consult any publication on project planning and control. See, for example, A. Baltersby, *Network Analysis for Planning and Scheduling,* Macmillan, London, 1964.

objectives, anticipated benefits, intended methods of approach, and its proposed implementation schedule. Secondly, the manager should assess both individual and group reactions after their questions, beliefs, and fears about the change are satisfactorily dealt with.

This can only be achieved by making the communication of the change a two way process. The manager must elicit comments and suggestions from the employees concerned. He must allow for sufficient discussion opportunities to communicate the rationale of the change and get the necessary feedback and suggestions from the employees. When a change is complex, and has far reaching implications, the manager should plan his implementation schedule so that sufficient time is allowed for discussions and other communications to take place.

Action to remove cultural barriers, mistaken notions and irrational fears can best be initiated during the communication phase of a change. This lays the necessary foundation for getting acceptance to a method of accomplishing the desired objectives of the change.

Gaining acceptance of the method of change

A manager can get agreement on a particular method of change in various ways. He can offer rewards or use persuasion. Alternately, he can negotiate and bargain with the representatives of the employees. Or he can encourage people to participate in arriving at the best mode of accomplishing the change. Finally, the manager can use any combination of these approaches. The particular approach to be used would depend upon the circumstances of each situation. Persuasion or rewards may be appropriate for situations where the manager is faced with only one particular method for effectively achieving the desired change. Negotiations and bargaining may be required to gain acceptance, especially if there is a union involved and the change is relevant to a labor agreement. Participation of the employees is most desirable when it is possible to achieve the change in a variety of ways. This invariably proves very rewarding, as it helps the manager to choose a method of implementation which causes the least resistance.

Whatever approach is used by the manager, he is likely to come across special personal problems from some of the employees concerned. The manager can overcome such problems by remaining sufficiently flexible in his attitude and approach. Exceptions and modifications to meet individual needs may be made to overcome genuine disparities which may be unfair to some employees. These will be accepted by the group if they understand and perceive the exceptions as reasonable.

The effectiveness of the approach the manager takes generally depends upon how much discussion takes place. Discussions should begin at the start of the communication phase, and should continue until agreement is reached on how to proceed with the actual transition.

Once acceptance has been gained from most employees regarding the method of implementing the change, the manager can confidently get into the task of its actual implementation.

Making the initial transition

At the start of the initial transition from the existing to the new conditions, the manager should review the timed plan for the change. He should consider whether it is desirable and possible to test the method of implementation on a trial basis. This can be done by either having a trial area or group, or by establishing a trial period. It is generally desirable to do this for complex changes where the outcomes cannot be realistically estimated. Such a trial provides an opportunity to test and experience the effects of the change, before it is made permanent. It can serve to modify the change, and can help to implement it successfully in its new form. On the other hand, where there is clear desirability and acceptance of a change, the manager should implement the change in its entirety. Alternatives and improvements can always be made in such instances later or whenever desirable.

Once the manager has finalized how the transition is to take place, he has to see that everyone involved is briefed on what is to take place and who is to do what. The briefing should help the employees to establish what their roles will be during the transition period and in the new situation.

If the change requires new knowledge and skills, then training activities must be planned and carried out. This will not only help the employees to carry out their new responsibilities efficiently, but will also help to reduce any fears and doubts which they may have about their new responsibilities. This training, if warranted, should be imparted to all involved—right from the managerial to the operative or clerical level. In complex changes, sufficient time must be scheduled for such training to be completed before the change is implemented.

Supervision has to be more thorough during the period of transition than otherwise. The manager must remain continually informed about what is happening at the scene of the change, and what progress is being achieved. To obtain a constant flow of timely information, the manager should employ various means. He should have his supervisors report to him daily on the progress achieved, and he should frequently discuss the situation with them. Staff specialists, if involved in the planning of the change, should be encouraged to contribute ideas, comments and assistance to its implementation. Where the union is involved, the progress should also be discussed with their representatives. Finally, and most importantly, the manager should pay frequent visits to the scene of action in order to gain first hand information about what is happening. During these visits, he should chat informally with those involved to get an overall assessment. This will enable him to take immediate corrective action, should that be necessary.

Consolidation and follow-up

The final phase in any change consists of the consolidation of the new conditions, and also the follow-up of events after the initial transition has been made. This phase should be continued by the manager till the success of the change has been ensured.

Even though the initial transition may have been accomplished smoothly, the manager should not presume that the change itself has been successfully achieved. There may be subtle secondary effects that may not be discernable for some time. Therefore, what may appear to be a successful implementation of the change at the outset may result in failure, due to the effects of subsequent reactions to the new conditions or because of other unforeseen factors. The manager can avoid this failure by consolidating the initial transition, and by following through to attend to problems and difficulties as they occur. He must remain flexible enough to institute desirable modifications in the way the change is being carried out.

After the finishing touches have been given to the initial transition, the manager has to employ a number of means to consolidate and follow up on the change. The manager should institute a procedure whereby he receives regularly scheduled oral and written reports from his immediate subordinates and from any staff specialists involved. These reports should compare the actual progress made regarding the change to the planned schedule toward achieving the objectives of the change. The manager should supplement this reporting procedure with on-the-spot visits and interviews with all categories of key persons directly involved in the change.

The manager's own first-hand knowledge, combined with the regular reports he receives, will enable him to evalute the extent to which the anticipated benefits and results have been achieved. If the objectives have been clearly defined, this comparison becomes both easy and informative. Such a follow-up procedure will reveal the existence of additional problems if they do exist. The manager can thereby act swiftly to either initiate further detailed investigations into the areas of difficulty, or to modify the appropriate elements of the change.

As a manager, by following such a systematic approach to making changes, you will be able to minimize people's resistance to change. This will be an important aid to managing people successfully.

Chapter 11

HOW TO KEEP CONTROL IN CRISIS SITUATIONS

It is often said that a manager's real worth comes out during crisis situations. It stands to reason that if you can handle crisis or emergency situations in a capable manner, you will be able to maximize your effectiveness in managing people.

Keeping control in crisis situations is facilitated if you formulate an advance plan or general strategy to tackle them. It is unlikely that you will be able to anticipate exactly the crises which actually arise. Nevertheless, anticipating possible crisis situations will help you to deal with the actual ones with greater confidence. Prior analysis of what resources could be used during various types of crises helps to handle them efficiently. Furthermore, you will be able to handle different crisis situations with fortitude and calmness once you have previously analyzed what, in general terms, should be done to keep control. Let us now review each of the considerations which will assist you in dealing with all types of crisis situations.

ANTICIPATING POSSIBLE CRISIS SITUATIONS

The first thing in planning to deal with crisis situations is to anticipate them. Since it is impossible to anticipate the exact crisis, it will be useful to think through the various *types* of crises which you are likely to face in your operations. Broadly speaking, crisis situations could be categorized as follows:

1. Crises regarding materials.
2. Crises regarding personnel.
3. Crises regarding finance and cash flow.
4. Crises regarding operations—equipment, procedures, electrical failures, etc.
5. Crises regarding miscellaneous environmental factors—fire, political unrest, labor union decisions, changes in government policy, obsolescence of present products and technology, etc.

Not all of the above may be relevant in your situation. But whatever your organizational responsibility, a few of the above categories would be pertinent. You may analyze specifically only those that you are likely to be concerned with.

While analyzing pertinent categories, consider the possible crisis situations you could be faced with. Then consider what reserves or alternatives you could plan for in advance to face such situations. Let us see how a purchase manager planned in advance to avert a critical material supply crisis.

Nathan D. was the purchasing manager for a large manufacturing organization. He had been careful to develop at least two suppliers for each of his major items. Nevertheless, he was worried about keeping the large factory supplied with basic raw materials and components, because of the recent spate of labor union strikes which had been threatening his major suppliers. It was practically impossible to maintain huge stocks of all such items because of the substantial capital tie-up and storage costs involved. Furthermore, the stoppage of supplies could not be predicted with any accuracy. Nathan anticipated a major crisis because of material stock outs, unless he made contingency plans in advance. He did two things. First, he developed the use of alternate materials, which were easily available, to substitute for the traditional materials, whose supply was uncertain. Specifically, he replaced some critical metal components with plastic ones, as the latter were available from cheaper and more reliable suppliers: Secondly, he got together with some of the local purchase managers to make out contingency plans. After about six months, a few of his large suppliers were suddenly shut down, pending labor negotiations. When this crisis came, Nathan was ready for it. The substitute materials proved to be of great help. Also, he managed to get some critical raw materials on loan from a neighboring factory, which happened to have a large stock of those items. On a reciprocal basis, he loaned out to them some items of which he had a sufficient stock. Some sections of his factory had to be laid off temporarily but, by and large, Nathan could avert the material crisis and keep the factory going. He could do this by anticipating the possible crisis situation in advance, and by making some contingency plans. His control of the crisis situation earned him the respect of the entire management team. It also got him an immediate salary increase.

Anticipating possible crisis situations in your organizational operations will help you to think of alternatives and reserves well in advance. This will enable you to plan ahead for meeting emergencies.

PLANNING AHEAD FOR MEETING EMERGENCIES

Having anticipated the types of crisis situations you may be faced with, the next step is to prepare in advance for meeting these emergencies.

Often, it is worthwhile to make out a detailed procedure in writing, listing what is to be done in an anticipated major emergency. This is essential for some crisis situations, like severe labor unrest, riots, thefts, etc. when they are imminent. Such procedures generally spell out clearly the steps to be taken in each emergency situation. They also have a list of important telephone numbers for getting outside help, as well as for internal communications. An excellent instance for planning ahead to meet a grave emergency is illustrated in the following example.

One of the manufacturing plants of a conglomerate was threatened with an ugly labor situation. The general manager and his team of department heads had been warned that they would be surrounded in the factory indefinitely if labor demands were not met. The general work force was ordinarily very peaceful, but outside elements had been responsible for exploiting it and issuing the threat. In some quarters of the factory, it was seen as an empty threat. Nevertheless, the manager in charge of administration was asked by the general manager to keep himself current with the latest developments. He conferred with the industrial relations manager, and decided to plan out a procedure to be followed if the factory was to be surrounded as threatened. A complete manual was prepared and circulated, with a step by step explanation of the procedure to be implemented by any employee surrounded in the factory. This also contained a list of all important telephone numbers—the police, government officials, the concerned industrial associations, and the corporate legal advisors. When, unexpectedly, an unruly crowd did surround the factory in a menacing manner, the necessary steps were immediately implemented. Within minutes, police were on the scene, and the legal advisor got a court order for dispersal of the mob immediately, as he had already gotten all the necessary legal papers ready. Before the situation could get out of hand, it was brought under control. Had there been no advance planning or an insufficient amount of it, there would have been an element of panic. The labor union had great political clout in the city. Had the legal maneuvers not been planned in detail, the police would have been ineffective, unless violence had occurred. In such a touchy situation, thoroughly contemplated and effective, immediate action is the only remedy. Last minute efforts can mean delayed action, during which time undesirable occurrences can take place. The administration manager's planning ahead helped to control a crisis which could have caused unnecessary violence and a shutdown of factory operations.

As the above example illustrates, in addition to anticipating possible crisis situations, it is necessary to plan in sufficient detail how to handle them. During the planning stage, the utilization of both outside and internal resources should be consciously incorporated.

USING AVAILABLE RESOURCES DURING THE CRISIS

Most managers in a crisis situation attempt to use the obvious resources available to them. These are mostly organizational resources, over which they have direct control. Unless they plan so in advance, it becomes very difficult for them to efficiently utilize external resources, or other organizational resources not directly in their jurisdiction. But the effective manager, who anticiaptes the use of internal and external resources in possible crisis situations, plans in advance to establish access to them.

He anticipates what resources may be helpful in need, and attempts to develop these resources. Thus, where beneficial, he will develop contacts with the government, social, economic and professional institutions, and various related individuals so that in time of need they are accessible. Similarly, inside the organization,

too, the effective manager develops contacts with useful resources
by establishing effective cooperative channels.

These contacts are necessarily dictated by the organizational
situation of a particular manager. One manager may need to
emphasize contacts with government agencies and officials because
of the nature of his work, whereas another may need to emphasize
closer contacts with financial institutions.

To best prepare yourself for using available resources during
crises, you need to take the following steps.

1. Anticipate what may be helpful in time of need, both from
   within and outside the organization.
2. Develop access to such resources through regular communications.
3. Plan to use these sources during the crisis on a reciprocal
   basis. This means you must have an understanding of mutual
   help and cooperation. This will improve the chances of help
   being forthcoming during the time of crisis.

When you are faced with a crisis, review the internal and external resources you have developed access to, and use the relevant
ones to help meet the crisis. Let us see how a production manager
used available resources to successfully overcome a crisis situation.

The production manager of a sewing machine factory had been
having quite a few technical problems. These stemmed from a
number of causes, chiefly related to the recent high rate of rejection
of stand assemblies by the quality control department. A crisis
situation developed when a large batch order of stands was rejected
by the quality control department. This held up a large shipment of
sewing machines, and put a huge order of sewing machines and
stands in jeopardy. Correcting the defective batch of stands in the
factory would have interfered with regular production schedules and
delayed other urgent orders. Envisioning a possible need, the
production manager had developed contacts with two large
workshops equipped to make stands and other sewing machine
accessories. He used these outside resources to get the defective
stands corrected. Because he had already developed such a resource,
envisioning its need, the crisis could be overcome without any ill
effects. The production manager loaned out some tools and dies to
the two workshops, and deputized one of his capable foremen to
assist in getting the batch of defective stands corrected within 3
days. Soon he was able to remove the underlying cause of the

defective stands in his own factory. Furthermore, he was fully prepared to meet any shortage in the production of stands for any reason, as he had developed outside sources of production to fall back upon. He could now face virtually any crisis situation regarding the production of the critical sewing machine stands.

In looking for an answer to meet different crisis situations available internal and external resources should both be mobilized.

HANDLING THE CRISIS

Meeting a crisis effectively requires that you remain calm. Although all crises demand immediate or prompt responses, nothing should be done without a quick, conscious analysis of how the crisis can best be tackled.

The steps involved in handling a crisis are as follows:

1. Avoid panic. It is essential to remain calm, but reflect forcefulness in getting the situation set right.
2. Draw out a quick plan of action, including what resources need to be used to overcome the crisis. If you are not sure of how to handle a situation, such as a complex technical problem, let the most qualified individual take over.
3. Implement the plan, and use both external and internal resources, as necessary, to implement a solution to the crisis. Wherever time permits, make handling the crisis a group effort.

While handling the crisis, your overall leadership will help to keep control. Nevertheless, it is important not to *insist* on your direct leadership in a crisis. If you find someone better suited to handle a situation with which you are not familiar, follow him. Support his leadership during the crisis, and orient your work group to follow his directions immediately. This will not diminish your overall leadership in the long run. Instead, it should further enhance it. Managers who have failed to do this out of pride, in a crisis which could be handled far better by someone else, have often further deepened the crisis and lost face. People appreciate an opportunity to lead if they think they are better qualified and can handle the situation better. Failure to give them such an opportunity will result in resentment and direct criticism, especially if the crisis is handled badly. On the other hand, recognizing their ability and allowing them to lead in a situation, with full cooperation, is likely to earn their mutual respect and admiration. Let us see how one manager handled a crisis best by passing on direct leadership to a foreman.

The new superintendent of production was responsible for the wood working shop of a large furniture making factory. An important step in the wood working shop was making plywood, which required the use of a large boiler. Within a few months of his new assignment, a severe crisis arose in the wood working shop. The boiler pressure controls failed to stop a steady increase in the boiler pressure till it reached the danger level. An alarm alerted the operator on duty, but normal procedures to reduce the boiler pressure failed to stop the steady rise in boiler pressure. Within minutes, the boiler was liable to blow up and send everything within reach sky high. Such an emergency situation had never developed before—in fact, this was a most unusual occurrence. There were no precedents to follow. Everyone looked up to the production superintendent for directions. There was one foreman who shouted that he was confident that he could handle the crises and stop the boiler from exploding. This foreman was not in charge of the shop, but was one of its most experienced workers. The production superintendent knew that the foreman had greater experience and knowledge than he did to handle such a situation. He told the foreman that everyone would follow his instructions, including himself. By a series of complete maneuvers requiring the help of the people around him, the foreman could start releasing the boiler pressure.

By allowing the foreman, without hesitation, to lead during the crisis, the production superintendent helped to bring the situation under control. Even a minute's delay because of vanity or putting on pretenses would have resulted in a major disaster. The foreman was amply rewarded, and was grateful to the production superintendent for having been given the chance to show his expertise.

In handling a crisis, the available resources must be utilized in an optimum way, without dilution. The focus must remain on how to solve the pressing problem with a team approach—led by the manager himself, or by a clearly more proficient individual.

FOLLOWING THROUGH TILL NORMALCY IS REACHED

After a crisis has been averted, it is necessary to see what its cause was and how its recurrence could be avoided. It is always a good practice, therefore, to follow through after implementing the immediate solution to ensure that normalcy is reached and will be maintained. In the previous example, the production superintendent followed through to get boiler experts to analyze what caused the clogging and pressure build-up. The results showed that the continuous use of extra hard water had contributed to the dangerous situation. He saw to it that a small water softening tank was installed. He also got additional safety equipment installed in excess of the equipment legal requirements. Not only did he follow up to see that normalcy was reached in the wood working shop, but he also made sure that such a crisis would not occur again.

Following through on a crisis is a critical step. Failure to do so has resulted in crisis recurrences in more severe proportions. This is illustrated by the following case of a not so thorough accounts manager.

The accounts manager of an engineering organization found himself being held responsible for a strong labor agitation. The labor union had threatened to strike unless the delays in the newly computerized payroll system were eliminated. The agitation had started when a notice was put up that due to problems in the new system, the payroll would be delayed. This had evoked a strong protest, and pressure was put on the accounts manager to get people to work overtime to manually get the payroll out in time. The accounts manager got the general manager's okay to do this, and brought the situation under control. Fifteen people worked through the night and got the payroll out in time. The accounts manager warned the computer section to see that this didn't happen again. But after two months, it did happen again, only with a worse mix up in the data fed into the computer. The accounts manager nearly lost his job. Because of his long service, he was merely demoted and put under a very capable administration manager. The accounts manager had failed to follow through the earlier crisis. He did not understand the root cause of the delay, and did not make sure that it was removed to establish normalcy. He had only solved the problem temporarily, and had not followed up to ensure normalcy of payroll operators. Had he done this, he would have discovered that the complex data on the production and efficiency bonus being punched in was susceptible to gross errors under the present procedure. Both the procedure of data input and the format of the final printout needed to be changed. This would have avoided the delays caused by errors to which the system was susceptible. Saving on the little follow-up effort to ensure normalcy cost the accounts manager dearly. He lost his organizational reputation, which would take him a long time to redeem. The more thorough administrative manager had never worked with computers before. Nevertheless, he not only solved the immediate problem, but went into details of why the payroll errors and consequent delays occurred. By doing this, he was able to initiate remedial measures which restored normalcy to the payroll system.

Oftentimes, a problem or crisis seems to be over when it really is not. It is not enough to pass on responsibility to other organizational groups. Personal follow up must be done to see that the crisis does not occur again. This is the only way to ensure that normalcy is reached.

By analyzing the different aspects of how to handle the crises situations discussed here, and by relating them to your own particular situation, you will be able to effectively manage people under the most trying circumstance—during a crisis.

Chapter 12

HOW TO MANAGE PROBLEM PEOPLE

Every manager gets his share of "problem" people. These are people who do not perform their job in a satisfactory manner, and impede the achievement of organizational objectives.

Being able to recognize such people and deal with them effectively can help you to appreciably improve the overall performance of your work team.

Progressive managers are directing their efforts more and more towards developing the problem employee, and helping him to become a satisfactory and desirable member of a work team.

Before one can solve a problem efficiently, one must understand it fully. Thus, before you can successfully manage problem people, you need to know who they are and why they behave as they do.

PINPOINTING PROBLEM PEOPLE

All problem people in an organizational group can be categorized into one of the following three categories.

1. Those who do not perform satisfactorily.
2. Those who are uncooperative and impede team work.
3. Those who break organizational rules and codes of ethics in a severe and/or consistent manner.

The reason why your problem people do not perform, are uncooperative, or break rules is worth analyzing. The egos of some people drive them to do individualistic and detrimental activity. Such individuals tend to be uncooperative. Mental slowness and sheer laziness can be other causes of problem people. Lastly, insufficient background, skill or education, or an unhealthy attitude towards work, can make an employee a problem case.

You can categorize your problem people in the three groups mentioned above. For each problem employee so categorized, you can then analyze the reasons which contribute to his problem behavior. These may be ego, mental slowness, laziness, insufficient background and skill, improper job assignment, work attitude, health, financial debt, personal habits, etc. Once you have thought through who your problem people are, and what some of the reasons for their unsatisfactory behavior are, you can then plan to deal with them effectively. A key factor in handling existing or potential problem people is to encourage them to discuss problems freely.

ENCOURAGING PEOPLE TO DISCUSS PROBLEMS FREELY

A lot of employees could have been saved from becoming organizational burdens had their manager been open to listening to their problems. Therefore, both as a cure and a preventive measure, you have to encourage your work group to discuss problems freely amongst themselves and with you. How can this be done? You can encourage people to air their problems by taking the following steps:

1. *Keep an open door policy.* This is easier said than done. A lot of managers think that they maintain an open door policy, but in actuality their subordinates are either afraid or think it not worthwhile to discuss their problems with them, as they know nothing beneficial will result from it. An open door policy is practical and will work only if the manager keeps an open mind, too. This means not criticizing or prejudging what others have to convey. It also means not passing the buck, and doing something constructive wherever possible to set right a problem situation. An example will serve to illustrate how one manager implemented an open door policy, and saw to it that it worked.

A well reputed organization's top management advocated an open door policy for all employees. Each manager was encouraged to lend an ear and make it possible for any employee in his work group to communicate freely with him. Though this policy existed on paper, very few managers were really regarded as being open to employee problems. Others merely gave lip service to the policy. John L. was one of the managers reputed to manage his people well. His subordinates could communicate freely with him, and he had been known to make good workers out of people who had caused problems in other assignments. In fact, some "problem" people from other departments had been transferred to his department, and had been performing well since. John took the policy of keeping an open door to employee problems and suggestions a little more seriously than some of the other managers. In order to encourage people to discuss their problems freely, he had a brief department meeting at the beginning of every month. This was an open forum where anyone could voice a suggestion and bring up a problem for group solution. Some months the meeting lasted only 15 minutes. Other months it went up to two hours. John also used the opportunity provided by the meeting to voice his own thoughts about the department's performance, how it was doing, and what required a little more emphasis in the coming month, etc. All his subordinates knew that they could air their difficulties and problems at such meetings. Nevertheless, there are always some employees who hesitate to express themselves in front of a group. John encouraged his people to discuss their problems individually with him, too. To avoid time wasting sessions, he asked his people to come prepared with relevant facts and figures, wherever applicable, when they wanted to discuss a problem. John heard out each of the people who came to him fully, without interruption. He had learnt that a premature response to cut short an employee who had not finished all that he had to say often left the employee dissatisfied. John took the time to counsel unsatisfactory or marginal performers on how they could improve their work. Quite often, hearing them out made it clear that they needed to be assigned to some other responsibility, in which they had greater interest and proficiency. More importantly, John had a cardinal rule with regard to discussing problems with his people. He made sure he responded to each genuine problem by either alleviating or removing it. His people knew that if they discussed a problem with him, something would be done about it. This motivated his people to discuss problems freely with him, thereby assisting him in managing them better. This was reflected in the high grade of work accomplishment achieved by his department.

An open door policy toward employees must be adopted to suit your own particular situation. It should not only be existent in name, but in practice as well.

2. *Encourage group discussions.* Another excellent means of getting people to discuss problems freely is to provide such a forum in group meetings. These meetings may be called occasionally to discuss a particular organizational situation, or may be called on a regular basis for reviewing performance and discussing problems facing individuals or subgroups of employees. Such discussions tend to increase cooperation amongst the group, and make the group much more effective.

Let us see how providing an opportunity to discuss a critical problem freely, in a group, helped a manager to handle a difficult situation effectively.

> Bill G. managed the sales department of a machine tools factory. He had been having problems in retaining his people. Most of those that did not leave had become problems in themselves, as they did not perform well. The efficiency of the sales department was low indeed. Bill knew from different individuals in his work team that they did not get the necessary support from the design and production departments to meet customer change requests and be competitive in the market. The production and design departments went strictly by the rules, and sometimes Bill had to go to the general manager to get their cooperation. On the other hand, the production and design departments had a few bones to pick with sales, and felt that they did not understand technical limitations and were un-cooperative. Employees on both sides were becoming thick-skinned. The sales force was not motivated to stretch itself to increase sales. Bill discussed this unhappy situation at length with his boss, the general manager. They agreed that it was necessary to establish a special forum for free discussion of mutual problems, on an in-terdepartmental basis, every month. Bill complemented this move in his department by having weekly work group meetings to provide an opportunity for a frank discussion of operating problems and critical situations. People who were becoming frustrated and tired of the existing situation voiced their feelings openly in these weekly meetings. Group discussions helped to increase mutual un-derstanding, and a number of minor problems were resolved through ideas brought out during these discussions. After a few weeks of these free discussion forums, Bill's work group suggested a change in order taking procedure and the input provided for production planning. Interestingly, some of the poor performers had some very good suggestions, which were matured in the group discussions and put into effect in a practical manner. One of these suggestions, which was immediately implemented, was for all the

sales force to receive special training in the factory. This helped sales to understand the factory's technical capacities for different products and to know what last minute changes were possible, and which were not.

As a result of the interdepartmental monthly discussions, a new sales ordering and production planning procedure was jointly arrived at, alleviating the difficult and frustrating situation which had developed over time. The group meetings were continued, because their usefulness as forums to discuss operating problems freely had been established. In his work group meetings, Bill did not leave it up to the outspoken employees alone to dominate the discussions, which is generally the case. He asked each employee, by name, if they had anything to say. This ensured that even the more subdued and reticent employees were encouraged to discuss their problems.

Establishing a practical means of encouraging people to discuss problems freely, on an interdepartmental and work group basis, had helped to change organizational problem people into members of an efficient, cooperative endeavor.

Appropriate group discussions can be very important in reducing organizational frustrations of employees. A somewhat related means of encouraging people to discuss interpersonal problems freely is through their participation in "T-group" sessions.

3. *Utilize "T-group" sessions wherever possible.* The third step in getting people to discuss organizational problems freely is to utilize "T-group," or sensitivity training sessions. We have already discussed this very successful, modern approach to work group and individual development. The purpose is to establish a free means of communication between the people taking part in the sessions, so that they can understand themselves and others better. The result is an increased sensitivity and appreciation of interpersonal relationships in the work situation. Problems are thereby thoroughly discussed in the proper perspective, and in a frank and free manner.[1]

The benefits of "T-group" sessions are manifold. They serve to (1) initiate individual employee development, (2) develop

---

[1] For a stepwise and illustrated approach to organizing T-group or sensitivity sessions in an organizational environment, please refer to sections titled "Starting the Development of Your Subordinates," and "Using Sensitivity Training to Improve Working Relationships," in Chapters 8 and 4 respectively.

cooperative behavior, (3) bring interpersonal problems to light, and (4) help correct problem people. In Chapter 4, we saw how Hank West took advantage of the opportunity to have "T-group" sessions for his work team. These sessions clearly resulted in developing cooperative behavior in his people, and served to bring interpersonal problems to light. That was the express purpose of having the sensitivity training sessions. Individual employee development was incidental. In another situation, a manager utilized the sensitivity training session to help develop employees both individually and as a group. Let us see how these sessions helped some problem employees to discuss their feelings openly and overcome their handicaps.

Peter L. managed the industrial relations and personnel department of an organization manufacturing electronic components and products. Though he had been careful to get suitable personnel for his department, he knew that most of them needed to develop themselves individually to better handle their jobs. In fact, some of them were considered "problem" employees by him, as they got tongue-tied in difficult situations and became completely ineffective. He wanted to increase the sensitivity of his people to interpersonal problems and further develop their ability to explain and discuss various issues with outsiders, union representatives and corporate employees. Sometimes, problems had been created when his staff had dealt with a situation tactlessly, or when, in his absence, one of his people couldn't explain an aspect of personnel policy very well to an irate employee.

Peter had heard of sensitivity training as a means of making people sensitive to their individual developmental needs. He got in touch with a management consultant who had conducted sensitivity training sessions, to find out if they could be arranged for the employees of his department. Although work group sessions were a new development, he was happy to know that they could be arranged. It was decided to have three hour sessions, once a week, for about four weeks.

The first meeting was disappointing. Employees had expected that there would be some sort of programmed instruction, but had found none. They were told that all meetings would be informal, and that they would have to bring up their own subjects or topics of common interest to discuss. Furthermore, anyone could initiate a discussion by group agreement. The management consultant clarified his role merely as an observer and coordinator of the sessions. There was very little discussion as such in the first session. Some employees said that all this seemed to be a gross waste of time.

In the second session, a poll was taken by the group as to what topics should be discussed. Out of frustration, a wide variety of subjects ranging from politics to employee benefits were suggested. The group majority rejected some topics, and allowed discussions to be held on a few topics. This included discussion on problems faced by individuals on a day to day basis.

The management consultant seemed to be passive and let the group go the way it wanted. Some active members in the group dominated the discussions. After a while, however, the quiet members of the group were asked by one of the supervisors to express their viewpoints as well. In the third session, discussions on organizational topics of common interest were allowed to continue for about an hour. Then the management consultant distributed a general knowledge quiz, first to be completed individually, and then to be tackled in group fashion by dividing the group into two parts. It was found that in one subgroup, the group effort produced a higher score than any individual score in the group. In the other subgroup, it was found that two individuals had higher scores than the group score. Obviously, the first subgroup had demonstrated better team work than the second. These exercises helped to highlight some of the problems in group cooperation and maximization of effort. Some individuals were surprised to see other colleagues do better than they were expected to.

The last session was devoted to an analysis of the demonstrated strengths and weaknesses of each individual. First, a general list of individual desirable strengths and undesirable shortcomings, relative to the department's needs, was made. Then, each individual employee was discussed in turn. By this time, rapport had been established, and each individual had begun to see how a group review would help him to plan his own development. Against each individual's name, the group was asked to express what they felt were his strengths and weaknesses. Then, the individual concerned was asked to express what *he* felt were his strong and weak points. This helped each individual compare how others saw him with what he thought of himself. The importance of how others perceived an individual, over how he perceived himself, was effectively brought out. The last session was very illuminating to most individuals. Each employee now understood somewhat the feelings he aroused in others, and why. The list of projected strengths and weaknesses helped each individual to see where improvements were needed. The sessions themselves helped to change a few individuals appreciably for the better. There was one employee who had never discovered for himself that he could lead a group discussion. In the course of these sessions, he had been asked to do so. He was certainly a changed individual. He had developed the self-confidence to express himself during these sessions, whereas earlier he had always doubted his own capability to do that. Another interesting effect was that individuals now felt that they knew each other much more intimately than ever before. The result was that interpersonal problems were discussed more freely, which made the department much more effective in its organizational role. Peter L. had successfully utilized T-group sessions to initiate the development of his people and give them the confidence and understanding to discuss problems freely.

Depending upon your particular organizational situation, you can use "Keeping an open door policy," "Encouraging group discussions," and "Utilizing T-group sessions" in any suitable combination to encourage your people to discuss problems without hesitation.

DEALING WITH PROBLEM PEOPLE DAY TO DAY

The biggest hurdle in dealing with problem people is caused by emotion. The problem person is often an emotionally ridden individual, who will generate emotions in you as well—generally of a negative nature. You will have to control your feelings before you can handle him effectively. Experience has shown that you can profit by the following four step approach in dealing with problem people:

1. *Control your emotions.* Very often, problem people are created by the force of negative emotions from other people. Good behavior begets good behavior. Never resign an employee permanently to the "problem" category. Approach every situation without bias. Give people, who have been problems in the past, opportunities to change for the better, in order to get the recognition or esteem they may be frustrated about. Do not try to hurt their ego—problem people are overly sensitive to matters of pride.

On the other hand, do not pretend to be too nice or considerate, either. Most people do not like charitable behavior towards them. They like to stand on their own feet.

2. *Give importance to individual feelings.* No one can confidently introduce a desirable change in an individual without un-

derstanding what his emotional needs are. Therefore, the emotions of the problem person are important if you want to change his behavior. This can be done by looking at the situation from his point of view, rather than your own. Then only can you appeal to what is important enough to him to change his behavior for the better.

3. *Learn the other's side of the story.* In addition to understanding the problem person's emotions, it is necessary to learn about his work constraints and day to day operational problems.

4. *Get mutual agreement on principles of revised behavior.* The next step is to get mutual agreement on improved behavior and performance. This mutual agreement may be either implied or clearly spelled out, depending upon the situation. In the case of ego or insufficient background cases, it may be preferable to simply imply the principles of revised behavior. Nevertheless, in the cases of mental slowness or laziness, it is generally better to mutually, and clearly, spell out rules of acceptable behavior and performance.

Let us see how a very successful manager followed these four steps in dealing with problem people in his particular situation.

The marketing manager of a gas range company had been unsuccessful in persuading the production manager to make certain modifications in the standard product, so that he could win an order from an apartment builder for built-in cooking ranges. In the past, too, the production manager had been reluctant to accept any order, except ones for the standard models or for very large volume non-standard items. His rigid approach had become quite a problem. The marketing manager knew that the apartment builder's order was non-standard and small. Nevertheless, he was aware that this would mean a large future order from the builder, if he was given the product modifications he wanted. The marketing manager wanted to avoid going to the vice president in charge of operations to get the order accepted, as that would further worsen the working relationships between him and the production manager. He decided to control his own emotions, and reassess the situation with the production manager. He tried to see things from the frame of reference of the production manager. He suggested to the production manager that a joint meeting with the builder's representative be held. This would enable the production manager to explain what could or couldn't be done. He stated that the production manager would be able to do a better job of this than he could hope to do by himself. Because he appealed to the production manager's self-esteem, he got agreement for such a meeting. The production manager suggested that the engineering manager be there as well. The marketing manager was glad to arrange that.

The marketing manager hoped that the production and engineering managers would be able to persuade the apartment builder's project manager to accept one of the standard models. Alternately, he hoped that the prospective customer would convince the production manager to take the job.

As it turned out, the two technical managers persuaded the customer to drop several of the more troublesome modifications and agreed to incorporate the less difficult changes. The marketing manager had finally learnt the way to change the behavior of the production manager. He regularized a procedure whereby he met the esteem needs of the production manager by encouraging his direct interaction with the customer for all non-standard product orders.

In the above example, the marketing manager dealt with his problem person, the production manager, by (1) controlling his own emotions, (2) understanding the esteem needs of the production manager, (3) allowing for operational difficulties, and (4) establishing an acceptable approach to handling order requests for non-standard items by introducing the practice of joining consultations with the customer.

This four step approach to dealing with problem people can be adapted to deal with problem subordinates who do not observe desirable forms of organizational behavior. The fourth step, in such cases, would mean establishing organizational rules to limit or discourage undesirable behavior. Thus, to avoid drinking, hazardous smoking, insubordination, etc. it is best to formulate clear-cut rules, if they do not exist already. When violations of rules occur by problem employees, you can impose a penalty from a warning to a discharge, commensurate with the situation. If there is a union contract, then the matter, of course, has to be dealt with through established channels. The significant thing to remember is that no matter what the rule, it must be uniformly and consistently applied; otherwise, even though an employee may be a clear violator, undesirable results may follow attempted enforcement.

A troublesome employee, who was discharged after her twelfth lateness under a company rule providing for discharge should an employee be late 12 times in a year, had to be reinstated with back pay and seniority rights. The arbitrator called the rule arbitrary and unreasonable, in view of a past practice of remitting up to 36 latenesses in a year and a system of warning now abandoned.

In addition to the danger of being challenged, a rule which is haphazardly or inconsistently applied will confuse employees, rather than curb undesirable behavior. It is essential therefore to see that rules are enforced in a consistent manner. Experience has shown that when dealing with instances of rule violations, formal written warnings bolster disciplinary systems in several ways.

• *The significance of the offense is brought home.* There is a powerful psychological effect in a formal written warning. It provides official recognition by management of the importance of undesirable behavior.

• *Consistent and fair enforcement is emphasized.* An employee cannot claim that a supervisor is unfair if he is shown that similar warnings have been sent to other employees, wherever applicable.

• *A better rating of the employee is made possible.* A complete record of warnings helps to rate employees with reduced uncertainty.

• *There is a greater likelihood of legal approval.* Arbitrators and law courts will more readily uphold a decision if the records show that the employee had received previous warning. A violater is often let off or draws a reduced penalty if he has not been warned.

Though formal arbitration applies only to unionized businesses, the general approach in handling difficult personal problems discussed here is equally desirable for non-union organizations as well.

REFERRING SERIOUS DIFFICULTIES TO HELPFUL EXPERTS

Sometimes the four-step approach, discussed earlier, to deal with problem people on a day to day basis may not work with people who have deep-rooted or serious shortcomings. This may be as a result of grave psychological aberrations, distorted personal perceptions, etc. resulting in advanced attitude and behavior problems. In other instances, a personnel problem may be enlarged out of normal perspective, and tend to become an explosive issue. In such situations, you can take the following steps:

1. *Discuss the problem person or situation with the*

organizational men concerned. It is a good idea to discuss serious personnel difficulties, as soon as necessary, with your personnel and industrial relations man, or his equivalent in your situation, in addition to discussing it with your boss. By the very nature of their organizational position, they will serve as helpful experts to assist you in handling the situation. A word of caution: Do not wait till the situation becomes virtually hopeless before discussing it with the personnel department and your boss. Alert them beforehand, as soon as you feel that a serious problem may result. This will get you their support and help if the situation does deteriorate and result in a grave problem.

The new purchasing manager of a light engineering factory discovered that orders for fork lift trucks were being manipulated by one of the maintenance foremen. This foreman had been with the company for a long time, and had good relations with all the key people. He did small personal favors for the senior managers whenever he could, in order to maintain good personal relationships with them. When sending in requests for fork lift trucks and parts, he used his influence to recommend what he wanted. Since the earlier purchasing manager did not understand or question technical requirements, the foreman had managed to get orders placed through a middleman at about twice the normal costs of equivalent brands. Obviously, the foreman was pocketing most of the difference.

Since ordering of maintenance equipment was done on a continuous basis, the new purchasing manager found that dealing with the foreman was becoming a problem. The foreman was very courteous and pleasant, but always dictated what he wanted, and got approval from the maintenance manager and the general manager whenever necessary. The new purchasing manager wanted to do things efficiently and economically. It was while reviewing the past files that he discovered that the well-known foreman had cost the company thousands of dollars extra in the past, and was still continuing to do so. He discussed the matter, before it became more serious, with the personnel manager and the general manager, and also mentioned it confidentially to the president of the company. The general manager knew the foreman for a long time and could hardly believe what he was told. In fact, he implied that as the purchasing manager was new in the position, maybe he didn't fully understand the technical needs of the maintenance department. The general manager, nevertheless, promised to warn the maintenance foreman and discuss the matter with him. The maintenance foreman, in the meantime, had learned about what the new purchasing manager was attempting to do. He countered with whatever emotional and technical support he could gather to prove that he was above reproach. The relevant papers from the maintenance file in the purchase department mysteriously disappeared. The foreman saw to it that through some of his friends, allegations were made against the new purchasing manager, saying that he accepted lavish invitations and gifts from interested suppliers. The president appointed a committee consisting of the vice president of operations, the head office general manager, and the factory's personnel and administration managers to investigate the incident. Because the new purchasing manager had discussed the problem situation with the relevant organizational people before it deteriorated into a fight for survival, his report carried significant weight. Had he waited and reported the corruption activity after allegations against him had been made, the report would have been viewed differently. The committee of internal experts which investigated the situation recommended the discharge of the problem foreman, and commended the efforts of the new purchasing manager in handling the situation with foresight.

Experience has shown that successful managers refer and discuss potentially serious difficulties with internal organizational experts as early as possible, and avoid waiting till the last moment, when help may or may not be forthcoming.

2. *Ask for the help of the revelant outside experts whenever necessary.* Some problem employees or situations cannot be effectively tackled with internal resources alone. Whenever desirable, helpful outside experts should be involved to resolve the difficult situation. Thus, psychologists, legal experts, renowned mediators and arbitrators, management consultants, etc. may be referred to the problem, depending upon the situation. Problem people with attitude constraints should be selectively sponsored for outside sensitivity training sessions, relevant management courses given by experts, etc., when there is a reasonable chance that they will benefit from these exposures. When a situation involves a problem group, then experts on group dynamics may be called in to organize beneficial group sessions to reduce organizational stress, and

to realign group objectives. In some situations legal advice, at the right time, can help thwart a bad situation from developing further. Outside mediators and arbitrators are often a great help, particularly when they are called in as soon as it is apparent that outside assistance would be beneficial.

A light engineering factory was involved in a labor dispute with its local union. The industrial relations manager and general manager had had several meetings with the union representative, but to no avail. A mutual distrust between the two parties had developed. Each doubted the intentions of the other of really implementing what he said. The industrial relations manager realized that outside mediation, by a mutually acceptable labor expert, would help in bringing about an early settlement. There was a labor expert available who had been a union leader himself at one time, and was now a well respected and renowned politician. The local union would certainly approve of him. The industrial relations manager knew that the labor expert could be depended upon for an equitable solution. He discussed the matter with him. The labor expert was very helpful and agreed to mediate. Since both parties trusted him, it was not long before an acceptable solution was reached to end the labor unrest.

Not all managers, however, utilize outside resources as well as the industrial relations manager did in the above example. Some managers do not even explore the possibility of getting outside experts to help. This is a mistake. Referring serious difficulties to outside experts is sometimes the only way a difficult personnel problem can be solved with the least damage and expense.

ADAPTING PROBLEM PEOPLE TO GROUP OBJECTIVES

One noticeable behavior, which most problem people exhibit, is that they tend to do things individually, disregarding group objectives. Because of ego, mental slowness, laziness, ineptitude or disinterest, they either cannot or do not want to work toward achieving group objectives. They therefore tend to be uncooperative. They only way to adapt them to group objectives is to appeal to their unfulfilled needs (such as self-esteem, affiliation and recognition needs) in order to motivate them to produce cooperative group behavior. This can be done in a practical manner by taking the following steps:

1. *Give their responsibility for meeting group objectives due importance.* It is certainly motivating to have one's responsibility recognized explicitly as being important to the group. By conveying to the problem person, in a suitable manner, that his work is important to the achievement of group objectives, you will be motivating him towards work accomplishment. For this to work, however, the subsequent steps must also be followed.

2. *Establish group goals and rewards which can be shared.* To motivate cooperative behavior, it is beneficial to provide goals and rewards which can be shared individually by the group members.[2]

3. *Let them feel they are wanted.* The worst thing to do is to treat a problem person as a villain. If you are working to adapt him to group tasks, make sure to give him the feeling that he is wanted because of the work he is capable of doing. Experience has shown that most problem people are victims of circumstances, and want to gain acceptance if given an honorable opportunity to do so.

4. *Provide opportunities for team assignments in which problem people are interested.* Assign problem people to areas of their interest. Let them join the committees or group assignments they would like to work on. This has to be done in a casual manner, as most problem people do not like to be treated special, since that would make them conscious of their shortcomings. By arranging to see that they work on committees or assignments which match their interests, you will motivate in them a desire for teamwork so that they achieve the things they want to do. This is known to help in improving their behavior in other areas of their work as well.

5. *Utilize T-group sessions to generate an appreciation for effective group dynamics.* If a problem employee is psychologically stable, his participation in a "sensitivity training" or "T-group" program will help to adapt him to work better in a group environment.[3] This will be an outcome of his exposure to group dynamics during the program. He will become more deeply aware of the impact interpersonal

---

[2] Please refer to Chapter 11 for a discussion on the impact of such an approach on employee cooperation.

[3] Please refer to Chapter 4 for details of how "Sensitivity Training" works.

relations and cooperative behavior have in substantially affecting group performance. Such a program is likely to make him more sensitive to group needs and adapt his behavior accordingly.

By following these five steps in the order most pertinent to your own situation, you will be able to provide a very strong motivation to your problem people to adapt their behavior toward group objectives.

CHANGING PROBLEM PEOPLE INTO ASSETS

There are four recognized ways by which you can change a problem employee into an asset. These are:

1. By *restructuring* his assignment so as to give him work he can handle satisfactorily.
2. By *relocating* him to an assignment he can cope with competently.
3. By *rehabilitating* him in his present assignment through promoting his individual development and providing supervisory guidance.
4. By *replacing* him with a person better suited to do the job.

The option to be exercised depends, of course, upon the situation and the problem employee concerned. To correctly decide upon the right step to be taken, it is necessary to isolate the negative factors responsible for the problem employee's performance and behavior. There are twelve such factors which are readily recognizable, and have a significant influence in causing undesirable behavior. An understanding of the following 12 factors is, therefore, important in order to isolate and resolve them.

1. *Job knowledge.* To perform well, an employee must have the necessary knowledge and skills at his disposal. When individuals are placed on assignments for which they are not properly prepared, performance will suffer until the needed know how is acquired.

2. *Family relationships.* Employees who have family disputes spend so much time thinking and sorting them out that their job performance is affected adversely. When family worries are carried to the job and necessary attention cannot be given to work assignments, a significant drop in performance level is discernable.

3. *Social values.* Some jobs require a highly developed sense of fair play; other assignments place a premium on aggressiveness. Job requirements that conflict with individual values create blocks, and thereby deter good performance.

4. *Supervisory support.* Poor supervision of individuals leads to poor performance. When support is withheld, and directions change frequently, poor levels of performance result. When supervisors do not organize and plan properly, employee effectiveness is affected.

5. *Physical fitness.* Employees must measure up to jobs physically. Significant health shortcomings may prevent employees from doing demanding jobs effectively.

6. *Living and working environment.* Some individuals are more sensitive that others to their surroundings. Climate, size of the community, recreational facilities, etc. cause problems in particular cases. Poor facilities, inadequate tools, and other substandard aspects of an employee's working environment also cause frustrated and undesirable reactions. Problem employees are often unwilling victims of their surroundings.

7. *Organizational policies.* In some situations, organizational policies may be too restrictive. Employees need a certain measure of operating freedom in order to perform effectively. Policies that disregard this need can result in dysfunctional behavior.

8. *Inadequate intelligence.* Employees must have the capacity to acquire needed knowledge and skills as well as to learn new things to improve their performance. When this is lacking, opportunities to develop are not of much help.

9. *Emotional strengths.* An employee whose emotional make-up is not in harmony with the demands of his work cannot perform satisfactorily. Before he can be effective, this mismatch must be removed.

10. *Group interaction.* When some individuals cannot get along with each other, the output of each person falls. Bickering, petty jealousies, rudeness and arrogance keep individual and group performance low.

11. *Inadaptability.* An employee who cannot cope with new changes in functional requirements often exhibits problematic behavior.

12. *Organizational identification.* An individual who doesn't support the objectives, goals, procedures and practices of the

organization he works for cannot get fully committed to its operations. This affects his performance adversely.

These negative factors, which generate dysfunctional behavior in employees, must be isolated and surmounted before problem employees can be changed into assets. In each problem employee, one or more of these factors are operable. How to surmount or resolve these negative factors is illustrated by the following case examples.

Case 1 (Restructuring Assignments)

Ken R. had been promoted to the position of national sales and service director of a large corporation. He found that his subordinate, Art G., in charge of sales and service for one of the product groups, was constantly having service problems. Art did a good job of organizing sales, but neglected service functions. This was becoming a serious handicap. Ken gave the matter careful consideration, and decided to utilize Art's sales strengths by restructuring the product groupings into separate sales and service functions, and placing Art in charge of sales. Another manager, Rod W., who had been responsible for sales and service for the other product group, was proficient in service rather than in sales, and was therefore given the responsibility for service functions in the restructured organization. Art and Rod, both of whom had been problem individuals in different areas, began to turn in good performances in their restructured assignments.

Case 2 (Relocating Individuals)

Bruce H. was a sales manager whose performance was adversely affected by his asthmatic condition. He had the ability but lacked the high energy levels essential for good performance. Realizing this, the vice president in charge of sales transferred him from New York to the company's branch sales office at Colorado Springs. There, Bruce's asthma disappeared, and he became one of the company's top producers.

Case 3 (Rehabilitating Employees)

John K. was brought in from a competitive organization to head the administration department of a large sales organization. He found that he had a problem employee in Tom H., who was the supervisor in charge of equipment order entry and control. Tom made many mistakes, and his day to day working was becoming quite a problem. John was thinking of letting Tom go and hiring a substitute. He checked to see how Tom had done in his previous assignment. He was a little surprised to find that it was Tom's earlier excellent performance in sales that had earned him a promotion into the administration department. Tom had been interested in an administrative position, and had therefore decided to switch from sales to administration. It was obvious, however, that Tom did not have any previous experience in an administrative job. John suggested that one of his top assistants work closely with Tom to give him continuous counsel and guidance, till he became more proficient in his new responsibilities. Tom was also sponsored for some seminars that would help him develop necessary administrative skills. This approach to rehabilitating Tom paid off, primarily because he had the capacity to acquire additional skills and knowledge. Within a few months, Tom became an asset rather than a liability for the administration department.

Case 4 (Replacing Individuals)

Bill S. managed the accounts department of a reputable organization. He had a problem employee who wanted to do things his own way. Bill knew that the employee was not an organization man. His analysis had shown that the problem could neither be solved by restructuring his assignment, nor by relocating or rehabilitating him. The employee was interested in the arts and painting. Bill advised him to devote his time more fruitfully in trying to do what he could do well, i.e., paint portraits. He took Bill's advice, and set up a small stall in the major shopping center of the town to make pencil portraits of interested shoppers. Before the problem employee left, Bill asked for the necessary approval and hired a person who could handle the job with greater interest and proficiency. This change proved extremely beneficial, as the department replaced a problem worker with one who did the work well.

These four examples illustrate how you can change problem people into assets. Your choice of the method would depend upon the situation and the employee's negative factors contributing to the problem. The four approaches discussed here can yield a high return with respect to the time you allocate to change problem employees into assets. Your success in managing problem people will depend upon how well you follow such an approach.